COÖPERATION

IN

NEW ENGLAND.

COÖPERATION

IN

NEW ENGLAND

By EDWARD W. BEMIS

BOOKS FOR LIBRARIES PRESS
FREEPORT, NEW YORK

First Published 1886
Reprinted 1970

STANDARD BOOK NUMBER:
8369-5369-X

LIBRARY OF CONGRESS CATALOG CARD NUMBER:
73-119926

PRINTED IN THE UNITED STATES OF AMERICA

TABLE OF CONTENTS.

COÖPERATION IN NEW ENGLAND.

I.

EARLY HISTORY.

BROOK FARM.

Coöperation in New England, if we except profit-sharing in the fisheries, began in the year 1842-7, when organized labor first became a power in Massachusetts, and when that remarkable enthusiasm for social amelioration was awakened which led to experiments like that of Brook Farm and Northampton. The same movement in France gave birth to Fourier, and in England to Robert Owen and the Rochdale Pioneers. The Brook Farm Community located about ten miles southwest of Boston, and the scene of an attempt (1842-6) to form a coöperative commonwealth, modeled in its last stages after the ideas of Fourier, was one of the earliest manifestations of this movement in New England. Although more ambitious in its aims and more radical in its revolt from existing economic conditions than most coöperative schemes, since it involved the whole social life, as well as the production and distribution of wealth, the influence of the experiment upon the subsequent development of coöperation was probably greater than is generally supposed. The saving attendant upon the concentration of the purchases of a whole community, equality of all shareholders in the management without regard to their amount of stock, and the endeavor to distribute the benefits among all, after payment of a stipulated interest on capital, were by no means the chief legacies bequeathed to subsequent coöperative experiments in America by Brook Farm. These ideas might have been, and often were in later enterprises, borrowed directly from England, or were a natural evolution from existing conditions.

The most enduring influence of the community was through its members, who were so stimulated by the ideas of Fourier, Brisbane, George Ripley and others as to become leaders and important contributors to the success of subsequent coöperative efforts. It is sufficient to mention as among the members John Orvis, of Jamaica Plains, Mass., and Jonathan Butterfield, of Wakefield, Mass. The former was subsequently the national lecturer and organizer of the Sovereigns of Industry, and is still a prominent, if not the chief, exponent and advocate of coöperation among the Knights of Labor in his State. Mr. Butterfield was for several years treasurer of the National Council of the Sovereigns. His brother-in-law, Mr. John T. Codman, of Boston, whose unpublished history of Brook Farm was freely used by Mr. Frothingham in his life of Rev. George Ripley, thus writes me:

"Certainly Brook Farm life was one of the early blossoms of the coöperative movement, which sprung from the clear heads and loving hearts of some of New England's best intellectual people, but like the early bud, it came before the frosts and ice of isolated winter had gone, and was killed. It showed, however, what fruit the future tree of life and society will bear—or rather what blossoms were in the innate life giving a harbinger of what the great future will develop of fruit in social and society life. I will say this: As a youth I heard all predicted of the present strife of labor and capital, and much more of what the future must bear of coöperation, or else the death of this nation is sure. As a youth I learned to reverence the great Fourier, the father of the development theory, whose great industrial ideas this nation is slowly reaching forward to and developing, without the thought that they are doing so—without giving him, or the Brook Farmers who tried to teach his doctrines, a word of credit. Brook Farm life and theories made me believe that industrial, and with it social progress, is the foundation of society and of our nation.''

The friends of Mr. John G. Kaulback, Jr., who is still living and head of a firm of wholesale grocers, 21 Central Wharf, Boston, claim for him an important place in beginning coöperative stores in New England. There had previously existed for an uncertain period the system of obtaining reductions in the price of goods for organizations that would pledge their members to exclusive trade of a certain store. Soon after 1840, Mr. Kaulback, then a tailor in Boston, was a member of the New England Association of Farmers, Mechanics and Workingmen, and deeply interested in its chief object, the securing of the ten hour law. Since the meetings were slimly attended, he conceived the idea that the members might be induced to come to the place of meeting, provided they could be made to see more plainly that it was their interest to do so. He therefore proposed that they contribute a certain sum individually, and therewith procure some of the necessaries of daily consumption and meet weekly to divide them. This was, at his suggestion, put into operation. A so-called dividing store was thus opened. From this small beginning, step by step, the work went on

2

until the year 1845, when the first protective union store was organized and commenced business.

After success was assured in 1849, the founders thus referred to this early period : "We were poor—a crime in civilized society—we were ignorant to a great extent of the arts and intrigues of trade, but saw enough to induce the undertaking of an experiment, and with faith in God and the right, we commenced our work by the purchase of a box of soap and one-half box of tea." Some dozen or more persons thus began in an upper room over the Boylston Market, October 6, 1845, declaring that their main object was the elevation of the laboring classes. "The dollar was to us of minor importance; humane and not mercenary were our motives."

THE NEW ENGLAND PROTECTIVE UNION.

An organization, called until 1849 the Working-men's Protective Union, and afterwards the New England Protective Union, was formed January 7, 1847, of the twelve local divisions then organized, of which ten were in Massachusetts, and grew so rapidly that in 1850 there were 106 divisions. The membership in 83 of them was 5,109, and the capital in 84 was $71,890.36, or an average of $855.83. The lowest capital was $150, and the highest $2,765.51. The sales of 73 divisions in the preceding year were $638,636.74, or an average of $8,748.44.

It was Albert J. Wright, recently State printer, now deceased, who first gave shape and form to the movement. Mr. Wm. F. Young, of Wakefield, informs me that Mr. Wright framed the constitution and laws of the New England Protective Union, and

later set forth its aims and purposes through a vigorous preamble, and was its secretary until succeeded
by Mr. Young in 1850, Mr. Kaulback meantime being
the Boston purchasing agent. The constitution of
the New England Protective Union, as of its off-
shoot in 1853, the American Protective Union, was
very simple. When fifteen or more persons, who did
not use or sell for use as beverage intoxicating
liquors, desired to form a division, they applied to
the central organization, which sent a delegate to
superintend the organization of the new division and
to designate its members. Local divisions were then
left to manage themselves, subject only to the following conditions: restriction of membership to the
strictly temperate as above, quarterly report to the
Central Division of the number of members, amount
of capital stock and any changes in its officers,
the payment of such small dues, rarely above three
cents yearly per member, as the Central Division
might require. Purchasing agents were selected in
Boston, and afterward in a few other large cities,
through whom the local divisions were expected,
when practicable, to buy their goods. These agents
had no salary, but could charge a commission of
three-fourths of one per cent. on purchases and two
per cent. on produce sold for the divisions. In the
constitution was this section: "The business of the
New England Protective Union shall be conducted
upon the cash principle. No credit shall in any case
be given. And furthermore, no division shall engage
in, encourage or countenance the traffic in intoxicating drinks." How far these provisions were
observed it is impossible to say. It is known that
some divisions gave credit and that many others sold

only for cash. In the early history of the movement
the practice was almost universal to sell only to the
stockholders and such other persons as were allowed
its privileges through charitable motives. After a
few years union stores were generally thrown open
to the patronage of all.

Although the founders of this movement professed
noble ideas of social amelioration, the majority of
the members were content with the practical object
of saving the expenses of the middleman and of the
credit system. It was recognized that the trader is
obliged to increase the price of his goods to cover
probable losses from the bad debts of improvident or
delinquent customers. The honest, thrifty purchaser
who is always ready to pay is thus forced to contribute to an insurance against loss from those who
fail to pay. No attempt to secure large profits was
made by the union stores. Dividends of six per cent.
on stock satisfied the members, and were often
declared. In many cases, however, no attempt was
made to declare any dividends, the surplus being
applied to increase the capital and enlarge the business, and thus indirectly increase the value of the
shares. Goods were sold as near cost as seemed
consistent with safety. The Sovereigns of Industry
claimed years afterward that they were the first in
this country to use the Rochdale plan of coöperation,
according to which goods are sold at market prices,
and all profits above a moderate dividend on stock
are returned every three or six months to the purchasers of goods in proportion to the amount of their
trade. I have found no direct evidence of the existence of this system in the union stores, but Mr.
Young, general secretary of the original organiza-

tion from 1850 to its dissolution in 1860, is authority
for the statement that coöperative stores on the
Rochdale plan were established in and near Boston
as early as 1864. The Charlestown store did a large
business and was successful for several years. Unfortunate changes in management and policy ultimately proved disastrous and caused its failure.
Very little public attention, however, was centered
upon this method of coöperation until its adoption
by the Sovereigns.

Great pains were taken in most of the union stores
to make them of far more general benefit to their
patrons than the ordinary joint-stock companies,
which they in many respects resembled. This was
done by limiting dividends and selling at small advance above cost. But the temptation was great,
and often yielded to, of increasing at the same time
the price of goods, and the amount of dividends to
the comparatively small number of stockholders.
Many stores thus ceased to be coöperative, and the
stock passed into the hands of a few of the more
enterprising or well-to-do. The growth of the union
stores prior to 1853 was astonishing. In October, 1852,
there had been organized 403 sub-divisions, of which
167 reported a capital of $241,712.66, and 165 recorded
sales the previous year of $1,696,825.46. No sooner
did success seem assured than union was changed to
disunion, and bitter dissension took the place of harmony. Many of the divisions, not seeing the advantage of buying their goods through one central
agency, and thereby obtaining the low prices attendant upon large trade, only sent to the Boston agent
orders whose filling was difficult and tedious, and on
which the three-fourths per cent. commission did not

pay the agent for his trouble. Dissensions thus arose. Other causes, doubtless, widened the breach, until in 1853 the old agent, Mr. Kaulback, was supplanted by another. This action was taken by the Board of Trade, which constituted the executive authority of the Central Union, and was annually elected by a delegate convention of the several local unions. The friends of the former agent rallied to his support and formed a new organization, with substantially the same constitution as the old, and known as the American Protective Union. This embraced for a time divisions in at least ten States. At its annual convention in 1857 it reported 350 divisions, with 327 of which the Central Division was in more or less close business relations. The aggregate amount of capital was reported at $291,000, and the amount of annual trade $2,000,000—its high-water mark, though a trade of nearly as much was reported during the next two years. Of the 769 divisions which either were in business in 1857, or had been previously, 46 were represented in the convention of 1857, distributed as follows: Massachusetts 22, New Hampshire 7, Vermont 6, New York 5, Maine 4, Rhode Island 1, Connecticut 1.

The original or New England Protective Union, though seriously crippled by the schism in its ranks, had reports in 1856 from 63 divisions, with 3,584 members, $130,912 capital, and a trade for the preceding year of $1,005,882.02. According to Mr. Young, about 700 of these stores were organized and went into operation. Though principally confined to New England, they gradually extended into New York, Ohio, Illinois and other Western States. Several were established in Canada and New Brunswick

and one in Oregon. Upon closing business most of
the stores returned to members the amount of original investment. In some cases considerable accu-
mulations were also divided. In a few cases, however, where the stock failed to satisfy the debts of
the store, the shareholders became responsible for
all liabilities, since most of the stores were not incorporated.

Causes of Failure.

Both organizations began to decline about 1858
and went to pieces at the outbreak of the Civil War.
"The uncertainty of prices at that period," writes
Mr. McNeil, "frightened the stockholders, and they
gladly sold to the storekeeper, who was willing to
risk something for the sake of continued occupa-
tion." Yet many of the divisions, as the stores were
called, continued business as independent associations. Mr. Wm. F. Young, than whom no one living is better qualified to speak of this first important
attempt at coöperation in New England, thus writes:

"There were several causes which tended to weaken and finally
break up the Union stores, such as lack of coherence and unity in
central organization, disposition to imitate and rival other stores in
useless display and expensive modern improvements, departure
from the original cash or ready-pay principal, so vital to all union
and co-öperative enterprises, and the want of proper qualities on
the part of those intrusted with the varied business details. The
sharp competition which sprang up between the union stores and
the retail dealers, which materially reduced the standard of profits,
contributed in no small degree to lessen the apparent advantages of
the system and discouraged many, especially those who gave little
thought to questions of economic reform, and whose attachment to
the organization was measured, largely, by the per cent. of immediate gains they were able to realize. The seductive cry of bargains
from the outside competition drew away many of this class."

The system of selling at cost, or just above, is
most difficult to follow successfully. We shall here-

after notice a few conspicuous examples of success in stores so conducted, but in nearly all such cases exceptional intelligence among the patrons, or remarkable capacity in the manager, will be found. The great weakness of the system is its claim to undersell all other stores. A fierce rivalry is thus engendered. A competition will offer some important line of goods for less than cost, and by well advertising this, persuade the mass of unthinking patrons of the coöperative enterprise that they can really do better elsewhere, though, in fact, a transference of patronage to the rival stores would, very likely, involve much higher prices on the whole of the month's trade. Another difficulty lies in the probability that, in trying to sell so near cost, unforseen expenses and losses will not only sweep away all profits, but also some of the capital.

The causes of failure have also been so well presented in Mr. George E. McNeil's report to the Massachusetts Bureau of Statistics of Labor of 1877, and the report itself is now so hard to obtain, the edition being exhausted, that I will borrow, to some extent, from his treatment of the subject as a supplement to Mr. Young's. The most visible cause of failure was the choice of incompetent managers. Men sought the place instead of the place the man. The case of one store where a good manager was chosen is typical: "For a few years all went well. Then began the whisperings of discontent. The management was arbitrary. It cost too much to run the store. The storekeeper's salary was too large. It was more than a mechanic's wages. The store could run itself. This man and that should be taught that others could do as well as they. By much whispering and

manipulation, many falsehoods and misrepresenta-
tions, the management was changed, innovations
were introduced, a new storekeeper employed. The
cautious were frightened and withdrew their money;
an unwarrantable dividend was declared to maintain
confidence, trade fell off, and they failed."[1]

People were then too self-important and untrained
in those habits of due subordination and unhesitating
obedience, which Therold Rogers considers necessary
to success in coöperation. This great difficulty, our
labor organizations, if they do nothing else, are
remedying. For, after all, the underlying causes
of all coöperative failures are lack of intelligence
and of the spirit of coöperation. Holyoake well
described the cause of many a failure, when he
wrote : "As soon as the sunshine of success warms
up the scheme, the envies and jealousies crawl out
like parasites, and in some cases when human nature
is worse than in others, they overrun everything and
make the society morally uninhabitable." All my
studies of coöperation serve only to confirm the ver-
dict of Mr. McNeil: "The failure of these experiments is not so much due to methods as to men.
The men are masters of the method. When it is said
that a store failed because it allowed credit, it only
half states the fact. Who allowed credit ? Not the
storekeeper. He was the servant subject to the
majority. It was a failure to coöperate, for coöperation needs an intelligence equal to the settlement
of such a question. If the management is charged
with dishonesty or inefficiency, the coöperators are
also responsible. The judgment necessary to select
the proper men is the first essential of coöperative

---

[1] Report of the Mass. Bureau of Labor Statistics, 1877, p. 125.

success. Men are often selected to important posi-
tions, because they are affable, agreeable persons,
qualities to be encouraged, but of little avail, if
methods of business are unsound."[1]

Survivals of the Union Stores.

There are now in New England three survivals of
the old union stores, viz.: at Worcester and Natick,
Mass., and Salmon Falls, N. H. Division 42, as the·
Worcester store is called, being the 42nd in order of
origin of the union stores, began in 1847 with about
$700 capital in $13 shares. Now the capital is valued
at $18,000, and none of the 130 shares brings less
than $150 when sold. From the beginning no one
has been allowed to own more than one share, or to
transfer stock save to the company. On the death
of a member the share reverts to the company for
sale to another, and the legal representative of the
deceased receives a sum equal to one share of the
net assets of the store, based upon the last report of
the directors. Either this provision, or the require-
ments that no stock shall be transferred without
being first offered to the company, is quite common in
the coöperative stores of to-day. The constitution of
Division 42 limits the membership to 150. Although
there are many desirous of admittance, only 130 are
now members, but the directors are considering the
propriety of admitting 20 more. As in the constitution of the New England Protective Union, no one is
admitted who uses or sells intoxicating drinks as a
beverage, or who is not of good moral character.
The applicant for a share must give two "good,
respectable references," must be approved by the

[1] Report of the Mass. Bureau of Labor Statistics, 1877, p. 125.

"committee of investigation" of three persons, and
receive two-thirds of all the votes, as well as pay for
a share. The profits, which go entirely to the stockholders, have varied from $5 to $50 a share. The
former was exceptionally low, and due to the expenditure of $2,000 nine years ago in fitting up the
store. The profits in 1884 were $35, and in 1885 $50
per share.

When the store was opened, goods were sold at
cost and no dividends were declared, but since the
present method of selling at market prices and dividing profits solely among shareholders was adopted
over twenty years ago, about $75,000 have been paid
to members. It is now really a joint-stock company
with stock equally distributed among 130 members.
By this restriction of membership and method of
profit-sharing, the store, which is very prosperous
with its annual business of $140,000 to $150,000, and
which occupies one of the best locations in Worcester
for which it pays a rent of $2,750, is not regarded
among the laboring classes of the city as truly coöperative. As its original members have died or moved
away, the high premiums for their shares, which
reverted to the company for sale, have placed them
beyond the reach of most. About twelve years ago
the private property of the stockholders was assessed
for $5,000,000, an average of over $3,000 each.
Despite the absence of many coöperative features the
original connection of this store with the coöperative
movement, and its continued success seem to call for
this notice. Its prosperity seeems due largely to the
ability and devotion of its manager, Mr. S. A. Pratt,
who has held his position from the beginning in November,1847, when he was employed at $1.25 a day.

He told the writer: "When getting $1,000, I was offered $3,000 to go to Boston, but I stayed, for I was desirous to see if the trade could be built up from a Christian standpoint. At one time I had my salary reduced at my request from over $2,000 to $1,500, when business was not very flourishing. I get whatever I ask, but I am not here to make profits for myself, but to build up a legitimate business." He spoke with pride of the fact that neither liquor nor tobacco were sold in the store, and that even the devotee of the latter would instinctively lay aside his cigar or pipe on entering. It is men of this manager's type of Christian manhood who are needed in all coöperative enterprises, and I may here confess that throughout my investigation, I have been most happily surprised at the number of such unselfish men in the community, and particularly in the coöperative movement. Two other important conditions of success have prevailed in this oldest of the survivors of the union stores, viz.: the general intelligence of the members, and the strictly cash system of sales. Very rarely is any credit given, and then wholly at the risk of the manager to some member of undoubted honor and solvency.

Second in age of the survivors of the union stores, though 108th among them at its organization, is Division No. 108, at Salmon Falls, N. H., started February 11, 1850, with a capital of $400, and now having a paid in capital of $1,705 in 341 five-dollar shares, owned by 202 members, and an individual surplus of $5,281.62, or a total capital of $6,986.62. No member can own over ten shares. The trade of the last three years has averaged about $48,000. Six per cent. dividends have been paid on the stock annually from the beginning. One thousand dollars was divided among the stockholders twenty years ago, and if the business should ever be closed up the present large surplus would be divided in the same way, according to the number of shares. The agent, Mr. R. C. Fernald, who has held his position throughout the thirty-six years' history of the store, writes: "We intend to regulate the prices of our goods so that the profits will just pay our expenses [interest six per cent. on stock being considered part of expenses]. We do not work to make money for our stockholders, but to save money by buying goods cheap." This has ever been their method of profit-sharing. Contrary to the usual practice among such stores, goods are sold to the 202 stockholders about two per cent. lower than to outsiders. Prior to the dissolution of the Boston agency of the New England Protective Union, about 1860, this store bought goods there. Since then purchases have been made of any wholesale firm. For the first twenty-five years a cash business was done. For the past ten years accounts have been kept, which the agent considers a mistake. As in the Worcester store a superior class of stockholders are secured, though they are not as wealthy as in the older store, applicants for membership must not only buy a share, but must prove to the satisfaction of the directors that they have "some visible means of support," "possess a good moral character," and are "of that class who honorably discharge their debts, and who do not make use of or vend intoxicating drinks," and any member, that is, any stockholder, may be expelled after due notice by vote of the majority present at any meeting for lack of any of these qualifications.

Any member withdrawing from the store may have his stock refunded to him within thirty days.

Another vigorous survivor of the union stores, although not started until after the collapse of the central Boston agency, is the Natick Protective Union. Organized December, 10, 1866, at Natick, Mass., with $2,000 capital in $10 shares, it now has $6,000 paid in capital in 600 shares, distributed among 575 share-holders. The par value of a share is still only $10, but the large dividends make the stock sell for about $30. The store was the successor of another Union store which had failed, and Mr. Isaac A. Flagg, who has managed the present store from its beginning until recently, when advancing years led to his giving up part of his duties, was a clerk in the previous enterprise. In October, 1868, only two years after its organization, the capital had doubled, and a stock dividend of $2,000 was declared. Some kept these extra shares, but many sold them and thus increased the membership. In 1875, under pressure of competition from the Sovereigns, 200 more shares were created, not to be sold to previous holders of stock, and only one to a man. Applicants for membership must not only pay for a share, but bring three vouchers, who are members of the association, and must be approved by the Board of Managers. Transfers of stock can be made to members, if they have not the full number of twenty shares, to which each member is limited, provided the Board of Managers are first given thirty days in which to purchase, if they so desire, but no transfers can be made to outsiders without the consent of the officers.

The object of the corporation is declared in the official act of incorporation according to State law

in 1866, to be "to reduce the cost of living." It had
just been discovered at the time of my visit, when
account of stock was taken, that the profits on meat
had been larger than expected, owing to a fall in
wholesale prices. Said Mr. Flagg: "We now sell
lower, for we don't want a large profit—we prefer
to benefit the consumer"—a very different ideal, certainly, from that held in our ordinary competitive
stores. Goods are sold to everyone, whether stockholders or not. Discounts on many articles of the
retail grocery trade are given to members, but low
prices are offered to all customers. Although prices
have thus been much lowered and consumers thereby
benefitted in this town of 9,000 inhabitants, yet the
575 stockholders have also been richly rewarded.
The profits on a ten dollar share for the past ten
years, including the regular six per cent. interest
provided for in the by-laws, have been as follows:

1875, $4.60	1879, $4.00	1883, $1.75
1876, 5.00	1880, 5.00	1884, 5.00
1877, 5.00	1881, 3.60	1885, 7.50
1878, 3.60	1882, 3.60	

In 1885 some surplus from the previous two years
was divided. It will be observed that in the last
eleven years over 500 stockholders have received
476.5 per cent. dividends, which is a remarkable ex-
hibit. According to State law, ten per cent. of the
net profits were laid aside for a reserve, until a surplus of thirty per cent. of the capital was thus accu-
mulated. This limit was reached at Natick years
ago, and all profits now go to dividends. According
to another provision of the State law, and according
to the practice of every coöperative company in New

England, each shareholder has a separate vote, without regard to his amount of stock. Groceries and meat are sold, but the accounts are kept separate, to determine the profit or loss in each. At first no attempt was made to solicit orders. Only heavy goods were delivered. Later, cards were placed in the windows for orders. Last year competition and the desire of the patrons compelled the use of teams for taking orders and general delivery as in other stores. Three teams are run and nine men employed. Three or four, however, are either too young or too old to receive full wages.

Full and admirable reports are printed yearly, which not only contribute to render the business safe and subject to the control of the members, but cannot fail to do much to educate all in business methods. From these reports the following totals of trade since 1880 are extracted—

1880,	$118,366	1883,	$113,996
1881,	123,153	1884,	105,600
1882,	130,081	1885,	100,176

There has been no diminution in the amount of goods sold, but only in the prices for them. The testimony to this effect among several coöperative companies is strong evidence of the reduction in the cost of living with respect to groceries within the last five years. At the time of the organization of this company, twenty years ago, some coöperative enterprises in the neighborhood had failed through credit; so this rock was avoided. There is no trusting, unless in small accounts for a few days, on the personal responsibility of the manager. The latter remarked that he considered it more difficult to manage coöperative than other stores, since the former must always be open to inspection and please everybody; "but," he added, "our members never trouble."

II.

THE PATRONS OF HUSBANDRY.

In 1873, '74 and '75 this order, founded in Washington, D. C., in 1866, spread rapidly in the agricultural portions of New England, and continues there as a well-organized and useful society. It does not seek or obtain much public notice, and a majority of those living in the cities are probably unaware of its existence. Its power for good, however, and its steady growth among the farmers, are none the less real. The order has grown in Maine from 7,039 members in 119 granges in 1880, to 13,531 members in 184 granges in 1885. There were in that year 5,500 members in about 80 granges in New Hampshire, and 2,500 members in 35 granges in Connecticut. The growth in Massachusetts has been from 1,141 members in 33 granges in 1881 to 4,078 members in 50 granges reported at the fourteenth annual session, held in December, 1886. The total membership in New England is between 25,000 and 30,000. The above figures are taken from the official reports and estimates of the various State officers of the order.

As the order was founded, and has done its greatest work outside of New England, it does not belong to this investigation to enlarge upon its history and valuable educational and social features. It is sufficient to state that the benefits conferred upon the membership in New England are as great as elsewhere.

3

GRANGE STORES.

In Maine the Patrons have several coöperative stores, whose success for several years bids fair to continue. Mr. F. A. Allen, secretary of the State Grange, writes: "I consider the outlook in Maine better than ever before." These stores, generally, resemble the union stores already described, selling goods at little above cost to Patrons of Husbandry, and the stock being owned solely by them. Some of these stores date from 1876 and 1877. Among them may be mentioned the Norway Coöperative Trade Association, organized in 1877 at Norway with a few hundred five-dollar shares and doing an annual business of $6,000; another at Foxcroft, Me., with the same business; one at Carroll and another at Belmont trading $4,000 each. Grange stores also exist at Samoin, Morrill, Jackson, South Paris, Topham, Freedonia, Dixmont and probably other Maine towns.

The largest grange store in New England is the Patrons' Coöperative Corporation, of Portland, Me., wholesale dealers in groceries, grain, provisions and farm supplies. Despite many letters of inquiry to the managers and directors, little information has been obtained. The capital of the store, which was organized in 1877, is estimated by J. W. Lang, of Bowdoinham, Me., member of the Executive Committee of the State Grange, to be about $40,000 in $5 shares, on which six per cent. interest is paid. The net earnings rarely permit much of a dividend beyond this. The State Grange owns about $4,000 of the stock. Many local granges have shares, and individuals own the rest. The store has a trade of about $175,000, supplying scores of grangers and grange stores with goods of all kinds at low prices.

The history of the coöperative attempts of this organization in New Hampshire are thus summarized in the annual address to the order in 1885, of Mr. Wm. H. Stinson, of Mt. Vernon, N. H., Master of the New Hampshire State Grange :

"In the earliest days of the grange, not only in this state, but throughout the United States, the financial feature was held out as the strong inducement for the organization. Every grange had its store, and patrons expected to purchase their supplies at wholesale prices. We also well know that these expectations were not generally realized, and the financial crash came, debts had to be met, members withdrew, and granges went to the wall. After a time the social and educational features were brought forward, the business item placed secondary, and on this basis the grange built on a firm foundation and grew strong and useful beyond the thoughts of its early advocates. The failure in business came through want of experience and proper adaptation to that work. Success follows experience, and failure that of inexperience."

The only coöperative store of any size of the grange, or as far as I can learn, of any organization in New Hampshire, until very recently at least, has been the coöperative store of Rochester. Mr. D. B. Waldron of Rochester, secretary of the local grange, writes that the store has $7,000 capital in the hands of 32 stockholders. All profits have gone to them since the establishment of the store in 1876. Goods to the amount of nearly $40,000 are sold yearly to everybody at just enough above cost to pay interest, not exceeding six per cent. on the capital. The store has been a success, thanks to a capable manager. Mr. Waldron writes that goods are sold in Rochester at the present time lower than in any other town in New Hampshire. I have found no granges in Rhode Island, or grange stores in Massachusetts or Vermont.

Grange stores exist at Torrington and Lebanon, Connecticut. Mr. B. C. Patterson, manager of the

Torrington store, writes that goods are sold only to members of the order, and at a slight advance above cost. It was started with no capital, but patrons furnished what little was needed at four per cent. interest, until the small profits repaid the loan. There is no stock. The funds belong to the local grange. Any surplus is used to obtain good lectures. and entertainments for the benefit of members and others. Only groceries are sold.

From Lebanon, Ct., Mr. Asher P. Smith writes that the grange store there has a trade of $16,000 annually. It has no share capital, but borrows $3,000 and sells at little above the amount necessary to cover cost and running expenses. The store is sustained by the 189 Patrons of Husbandry in Lebanon.

TRADE DISCOUNTS.

That elementary form of coöperation where the members of an organization buy at reduced prices for cash, by agreeing to concentrate their trade on certain stores, is widely prevalent throughout the order in New England. Secret circulars are issued to members giving lists of stores and discounts where such arrangements have been made. The goods on which such discounts can be obtained in New Hampshire, according to the official circular of 1886, embrace agricultural machinery, tools, boots and shoes, books, stationery, seeds, custom and ready-made clothing, dress and dry-goods, groceries, grain and feed, paints, furniture, sewing machines, pumps, and in fact everything needed by the farmer. The state granges of New Hampshire, Vermont, Massachusetts and Connecticut, have made joint arrangements with a large number of manufacturers and wholesale

firms for stipulated discounts on cash trade, subject
to certain conditions, viz.: Each subordinate grange
to choose one member as purchasing agent, all purchases to be made through him, and the list of the
houses making the discounts to be kept from the
knowledge of those who are not members. Confi-
dential price-lists are furnished purchasing agents
upon application, under seal of their subordinate
granges, and attested by the master and secretary
of these granges. Coöperative life and fire insurance companies are also being introduced. Mr. J.
H. Hale, of South Glastonbury, Ct., Master of the
Connecticut State Grange, estimates that from $40,-
000 to $50,000 were saved to the patrons in New
England in 1886, by these various coöperative forms.

III.
THE SOVEREIGNS OF INDUSTRY.
EARLY HISTORY.

With the first month of 1874 a new factor in coöperation appeared, which was destined, in the five
years of its eventful history to give a great impulse
to coöperative effort and to mark a great advance in
its methods. The history of the Sovereigns of Industry has never been written, yet not only to the social
reformer, but to all students of social science, the
story of its rapid rise, and almost equally rapid decline, is full of instruction.

The founder of the order, and for four years its
official head, Mr. Wm. H. Earle, was in 1874 a small
fruit-grower of Worcester, Mass. His five acres
within the city limits, located on a beautiful hillside,
sloping to the south, overlooked this picturesque city,

and here he still resides, though in other business, as
full of faith as ever in the future of the ideas to
which he gave some of his best years. The Worcester *Gazette* of January 15, 1874, thus referred to him:
"Mr. Earle has resided in this city but a few years,
but has won the respect and confidence of all with
whom he has come in contact. In matters pertain-
ing to horticulture, and among those interested in
that pursuit, he is widely and favorably known."
He thus relates the origin of the Order of the
Sovereigns:[1]

"Dudley W. Adams of Waukon, Iowa, (in 1872 Master of the
Iowa State Grange), was an old schoolmate of mine, and when he
became Master of the National Grange of the Patrons of Husbandry, he wrote me inviting me to take hold of the work of organizing granges in Massachusetts. I began carefully to study this
whole question of labor and capital, of producer and consumer,
spoke to some of our leading agriculturists and arranged to organize
a grange in our city. About the time we organized this grange the
question came up, 'Why should the Patrons of Husbandry refuse
to admit all but farmers?' The more I studied this question, the
more thoroughly convinced I became that, while the common foes
and common wants of all the toiling men and women in our land
were nearly alike, there was no good reason why all persons of
good character, engaged in industrial pursuits, and having no
interests in conflict with the purpose of the order, should not be
eligible."

Invitations were therefore sent about this time,
January 1, 1874, to different parts of the country to
such persons as were believed to be in sympathy with
such movement. A convention was called to meet
in Springfield, Mass., January 6th. At that date
some fifteen laboring men met to consult about the

[1 I must acknowledge my great indebtedness for the history of
the Sovereigns to Mr. W. H. Earle, who placed at my disposal
a mass of material, including the unpublished records of the
National Council.]

advisability of organizing a new society or order. For eight days and nights they earnestly discussed this question and a plan of organization, and then adopted a preamble, constitution and ritual, and organized as the National Council of the Order of Sovereigns of Industry.   The afternoon of January 16, the day after the adjournment of the Springfield convention, Mr. Earle organized the first subordinate council of the order at Worcester.   The same evening a council was formed in Springfield, Mass., partly through the instrumentality of a relative of the founder.   Other councils were immediately formed in other states, Mr. Earle organizing the first council in six states within a few weeks.   It was soon found that the movement was to become of far greater magnitude than had been at first expected, and "in order to lay the foundations strong and deep," writes Mr. Earle, he and his coadjutors were compelled to call a special session of the National Council to make certain alterations in the constitution and ritual.   These alterations were made at Springfield, Mass., March 5th, 6th and 7th, 1874, by representatives from most of the sub-councils then organized.   "At our first meeting in January," continued Mr. Earle, "we met as strangers.   I knew only one person in attendance at the convention, and had no thought of becoming conspicuously identified with the movement, but went because my heart was in the work.   Very unexpectedly I was unanimously elected president."   At the special session he resigned, and was again unanimously elected, and continued to hold that office by the same unanimous choice until ill-health compelled his resignation in 1878.

It is now time to consider the objects and methods of this new order. The purposes of the founders are so well expressed in the preamble to the constitution, and were so confirmed by the subsequent history of the movement, that one cannot do better than quote :

"By all the wise and kindly measures it can command, it will present organized resistance to the organized encroachment of the monopolies and other evils of the existing industrial and commercial system. It will try to establish a better system of economical exchanges and to promote, on a basis of equity and liberty, mutual fellowship and coöperative action among the producers and consumers of wealth throughout the earth. We wage no wars with persons or classes, but only with wrongs, discords and hardships, which have existed too long. We most earnestly deprecate hatred, jealousy or envy between classes, and call on all people to be of one mind in the spirit of justice. We abhor every scheme of agrarianism or violence, and shall use only such instrumentalities as are sanctioned by demonstrated principles of moral philosophy and social science, the universal interests of humanity, and a philanthropy rising impartially above all distinctions of class, sex, creed, race or nationality."

In the first address of President Earle to a subordinate council—that at Worcester—on its organization, January 16, 1874, he used these words : "I wish first of all to say that this order seeks to bring these two classes (employés and employers) into a closer fellowship of good feeling and mutual interest."

It was proclaimed that any person of "good character and having no interest in conflict with the order" could be admitted on vote of a subordinate council, and on payment of an initiation fee of $2 for men, $1 for women, and yearly dues of from $1 to $4, as local necessities might require. At the commencement, at least, lawyers and professional politicians were excluded, as by another organization of more recent fame, the Knights of Labor. In Massachusetts, and probably in some other States, three black balls caused the rejection of a candidate. The secret ritual of the order is a secret no longer, and contains nothing to which anyone could not readily subscribe.

Each subordinate council was entitled to two representatives in the state council, and the latter sent representatives to the national council which met once a year, listened to reports, legislated for the interests of the order, and elected officers for the ensuing year. Arrangements were made by means of traveling and withdrawal cards for members moving from the seat of one council to that of another.

Most of the councils began coöperation by empowering agents to buy for cash at wholesale prices, at regular intervals of a week or longer, such goods as the members of the local council deposited money for in advance. Thus without capital, goods were obtained at marked reduction from the high retail prices of that period. An annual trade of many hundred thousand dollars thus sprang up in New England, and much was saved to the laboring classes. Many, perhaps half, of the councils, never went further. The largest store of the order, and, with the exception of one at Worcester, which preceded it in organization by a few hours, the oldest store was that at Springfield, Mass. Its history is so full of lessons of warning that a brief account of its rapid rise and unfortunate ending may not be amiss.

THE SPRINGFIELD STORE.

January 16, 1874, as a result of the visit from Mr. Earle above referred to, a council of 26 was organized in the well-known city of the Connecticut valley, where lived at that time some 30,000 people. The Springfield council agreed to center its trade and pay cash at certain large retail stores on condition of receiving a reduction in price, a method of trading now practiced by the Patrons of Husbandry; but other cash customers of the stores began to complain, because they did not obtain similar reduction.   Several new councils were organized in the city and vicinity who contributed as councils $300 and empowered one of their members, Mr. O. S. Brigham, to purchase goods for them at wholesale, as in the dividing houses which had previously been started from time to time in New England.   Not a wholesale house in town would sell to Mr. Brigham for fear of a boycott, or, at least loss of trade from other stores.   So goods were purchased in Boston without divulging at first the nature of the company for which they were bought.   Before long wholesale dealers welcomed the agent of the Sovereigns, who came cash in hand. The goods were sold at just enough above cost to cover expenses.   Mr. Brigham charged nothing for his services, and each customer could inspect the bills to see the price paid the wholesale dealers. Trade increased so fast that a store was opened for the whole day, and a storekeeper was hired. The capital, which never exceeded $750 during the year 1874, was turned over quickly.   Flour was ordered by the one hundred barrels from Michigan.   The coal dealers of Springfield refused to sell below the retail price of $10 a short ton.   After considerable difficulty a man in Hudson, N. Y., was found who was ready to defy the combination of coal dealers and sell to the coöperators.   Six to ten carloads at a time were bought, the customers paying the price at the Springfield store when the order was left.   Coal was sold for $7 a ton instead of $10, and all the local dealers

had to fall correspondingly. Trade rose to $4,700 a
month. Scarcely any expenses were allowed. Customers were expected to take home their goods
or pay a small sum for carriage. Eighteen large
tubs of butter were taken away by hand in one evening. One man did all the delivering, except of coal.
There was no taking of orders from house to house
and no advertising. Trade was confined to the Sovereigns. The fee on joining was $2 for men and $1
for women; the monthly dues were 50 cents for men
and half that for women. As might be expected, the
order grew rapidly.

For greater security of funds it was decided in
December, 1874, to incorporate under the Massachusetts coöperative law of 1870, and the act amend-
atory thereto. A capital of $3,100 was raised and
subsequently doubled ; the stock and fixtures of the
old store were bought, and on March 10, 1875, the
new company began business. The plan of coöperation, which soon became famous as the "Springfield
plan," was a natural sequence to that of the previous
store, where goods were sold at cost and the capital
was furnished by the local councils. By the constitution of the new company the capital was furnished by the members of the order loaning to their
respective councils such amounts as they chose, and
receiving therefor the council's note, payable at a
specified time, with interest at seven per cent. When
a council raised in this way the sum of $100, it
elected, by ballot, a member to represent the money,
who, on behalf of the council, purchased a share in
the corporation, taking the certificate of stock in his
own name, but immediately turned over the same to
the treasurer of the council as collateral security for

the money placed in his hands. The corporation thus formed, elected directors who chose the managers and assistants in the various departments of the store, which were soon established, such as meat, groceries, clothing, boots and shoes. Sales, which were to be for cash and but little above cost, were confined to Sovereigns. As, however, the saving of $2 on a barrel of flour sufficed for a membership fee, the order seemed strengthened thereby. One of its officers wrote in November, 1875: "Our purpose is to save, not make money—and this we believe we are doing, or our business would not have so rapidly and steadily increased. Commencing as we did with a stock of only four hundred barrels of flour, some fifteen months since, we cannot but look upon our trade for the present month, amounting to about $13,000, with feelings of mingled pride and satisfaction." Seven per cent. interest was to be paid, and for a time was paid on stock. It was voted in October, 1875, that goods should be sold at a price sufficient to allow of profits not exceeding two per cent. on gross sales, half to be put in a bank as a sinking-fund and half to be given to the councils represented.

Business increased so fast as fairly to bewilder the directors. A new building, with ample accommodations for council meetings and stores, erected on purpose for the order, was dedicated with imposing ceremonies October 19, 1875, and leased to the Sovereigns for $2,400 a year.

The balance sheet for 1876 revealed receipts for sales that year of $134,813.73 thus divided : From groceries, $77,430.21 ; from coal, $18,405.81; from meat, $33,313.31; from clothing, $5,624,40—a larger trade than that of any other coöperative store of the

order, while the membership of the seven councils in
Springfield and adjacent towns was over 3,000. But
in this very prosperity there were seeds of decay.
By attempting to sell at cost, and claiming thus to
undersell every other store in town, a fierce competition, pronounced by wholesale dealers at that time to
be the fiercest in all Massachusetts, was engendered.
Some rivals would offer sugars below cost, trusting
to profits on other goods to recompense themselves.
Others undersold the Sovereigns on other staples. It
still remained true, doubtless, that on the entire
monthly trade of a family the coöperative company
furnished the best bargains, but the mass of customers, unacquainted with the principles of coöperation, and ignorant of how to make their experiment
a success, were led to transfer more and more of their
trade to private stores, and finally to withdraw from
the Sovereigns altogether by failing to keep up their
dues. As the store could only sell to Sovereigns,
while they could buy anywhere, trade began a rapid
decline.

But there were other causes of failure. The method
of raising capital by councils rather than by individuals was joined with a provision that the directors of
the store should be elected by the councils, and not
by those who in each council contributed to the purchase of shares. In consequence, very much such a
state of things existed as is advocated by some social-
ists, viz.: An industry managed by the votes of a
democracy, by far the larger part of which has contributed nothing to the capital stock. Whatever may
be the possibilities of such a system, the Springfield
attempt was a decided, and it would seem, inevitable
failure. Directors were elected, and managers and

clerks in the various branches of the store were chosen who knew nothing of the business. Carpenters and old employés of the United States Armory were suddenly transformed into managers and clerks of a rapidly growing and little understood business. At regular intervals the directors engaged different ones of their number, and sometimes fair book-keepers, to inspect the accounts of the various agents and managers in the store. Never, I am told by one of the leading directors, did any two inspectors or auditors agree in their report, or find any way of balancing the accounts. Each agent claimed to have a different "system" of book-keeping. Certainly, no auditor professed to understand the books. After the store failed in 1879, it was found that, contrary both to the constitution and the orders of the directors and without their knowledge, thousands of dollars worth of goods had been sold for credit and never paid for. It is believed on good grounds by some of the directors that dishonesty among the employés was also practiced. When the store was doing a business of $4,700 a month under Mr. Brigham, early in 1875, only two clerks and one team were employed. With little more than twice the trade more than ten clerks and six teams were employed two years later. The expense for labor in 1876 was $7,810.61, and for teams $1,023.51. The total expenses were nine per cent. of the sales, to say nothing of the depreciation of goods on hand. The trade expenses in 1,153 coöperative societies of the United Kingdom in 1883, reporting a trade of £28,089,310, were only six per cent. of their sales. What economy there was attempted was in the wrong direction. One thousand dollars were paid to the manager, but many thought

·even that too high. A mistake was made in attempting too many kinds of business. A costly, stylish lot
of clothing and caps were put into the clothing store
and met with poor sale. Attempts were made to
amend the constitution. After 1876 manager and
clerks were paid a fixed percentage on sales, instead
·of salary and wages. In April, 1878, trade was
thrown open to the public. Already in October,
1876, a committee reported in favor of changing to
the Rochdale plan of coöperation to be explained
hereafter, but the report was not acted upon until
1878, when a complete change was made in the
·entire constitution. The Rochdale plan was adopted
with sales at regular retail prices, and with a division of profits in excess of three per cent. on capital
among customers, according to their trade. The
$100 shares broken up into shares of $5 each were to
be owned by individuals. But it was too late to
·stay the downward course. On January 22, 1879,
the corporation voted to dissolve, having sunk a
large portion of its capital. Coöperation received a
blow from which it has not yet recovered in the Connecticut Valley.

Such is the story of many other misguided attempts
at coöperation by men too ignorant or selfish or dis-
united to coöperate. Yet the Springfield experiment
was not wholly a failure. It contributed largely to
induce cash trade and low prices in all this section of
country, and thus did incalculable good to the laboring classes. Said one of the directors: "Many persons to my certain knowledge, who had always been
behind, and thought they could not leave the old
store because they were behind, and whom I induced
to transfer their trade to the Sovereigns, lived

economically and paid their old bills out of what they
saved from cash trade with us." So little discouraged is Mr. O. S. Brigham, the pioneer of the Springfield enterprise, and now partner in a large wholesale fruit business, that, in answer to the question
whether he still believed a coöperative enterprise
could meet the keen competition and low prices now
prevailing, replied: "You give me one hundred
families who will be true to their best interests and I
will beat any store in town."

THE ROCHDALE PLAN.

The Sovereigns seem to have been the first to
introduce into America the Rochdale plan of coöperation, which has proved so superior to other forms
wherever tried, but which will not "run itself" any
better than other systems, as many have found to
their sorrow. The essential improvement of this
plan over others is in its provision that goods are
sold at regular retail prices, and any profits above
what is sufficient for a reserve fund and interest on
capital are paid to customers annually or semi-
annually in proportion to their trade for the period,
though stockholders may receive a larger per cent.
of dividend on their trade than outsiders. The other
provisions, such as shares of small value, limitation
of the number anyone can hold, and the allowance
of but one vote to a stockholder, independent of his
shares, are common to other systems.

In his address to the National Association at
Washington, March, 1878, President Earle thus referred to some of the superior features of the English
system:

"It is only by the exercise of frugality that the workingman
can be enabled to surround himself and his family with the com-

forts of life. Coöperation will not benefit him if he does not culti-
vate provident habits. It is because the Rochdale plan of coöperation encourages these habits that I advocate its adoption in preference to all other plans. It is found that of the seven and one-half
millions of dollars annually saved by the English coöperative
societies, about sixty per cent. of this sum of 'dividends on purchases' is left in the store and converted into capital."

Great efforts were made by the National Council
and by its lecturer, John Orvis, to spread a knowledge of the system of distributive coöperation that
had proved most successful in England. Under their
sanction, and to secure uniformity among the councils, a plan for the organization and management of
coöperative stores was prepared by John Orvis and
widely distributed, for $5 a hundred copies, which
might well be studied to-day by every one interested
in the subject. Only the omission of a few references to the now extinct organization of Sovereigns
of Industry is needed to make it conform to existing
conditions. In sending out the plan the National
Council thus summarized it:

"1. Allow but one vote to a shareholder, without regard to the
number of shares held.

"2. Shares to draw a minimum rate of interest.

"3. Dividends to be made only on purchases, and that quarterly.

"4. Every member of the order entitled to full dividends on
purchases, provided the directors may retain such dividends in
their discretion, until the same shall amount to at least one share
of stock.

"5. Shares not to exceed $5 each, unless required otherwise by
statute.

"6. Dividends to non-members one-half the profits on their
purchases.

"7. Sell at current prices—the same price to members of the
order and the general public—thus disarming opposition.

"8. Look after the interests of the store as strictly as if the
store were an individual property.

"9. Choose persons worthy of your confidence for managers—
then give them your hearty support."

4

It was also provided that the directors could obtain loans for the business of the association by a vote of three-fourths of the shareholders, and to an amount not exceeding two-fifths of the actual capital of the association. Shares could be transferred to any one approved by the directors, but must first be offered to them.

This was the plan on which nearly half of the Sovereigns' stores started, and on which nearly all that succeeded were founded.

SUCCESS AND FAILURE OF THE SOVEREIGNS.

Before describing any of the successful examples of the Rochdale plan in New England it may be well to finish our account of the order of the Sovereigns, which, in spite of its failure as an organization, gave birth to many existing coöperative enterprises. Annual sessions of the order were held from 1874 to 1879 inclusive. From the annual official reports at these sessions, and from the pages of the *Bulletin*, the official organ, which was published for two years in Worcester as a 16-page monthly paper, the following facts and tables are gathered. As it is useful to compare sections, and the matter given cannot elsewhere be found in printed form, I have in a few cases exceeded the proper bounds of this paper by including tables or summaries of other states—

State	1874 Memb. Rep.	1875 No. Rep.	1875 No. Supp.	1875 Memb. Rep.	1876 No. Rep.	1876 No. Supp.	1876 Memb. Rep.	1877 No. Rep.	1877 No. Supp.	1877 Memb. Rep.	1878 No. Rep.	1878 No. Supp.	1878 Memb. Rep.
Maine	552	19	29	1,518	28	48	1,801	24	30	1,051	10		580
New Hampshire	887	9	13	1,115	15	20	946						
Vermont	406	10	11	932	3	14	280				2		45
Massachusetts	9,767	117	155	12,137	60	131	4,024	48	91	3,428	18		2,118
Connecticut	4,855	30	49	3,816	14	38	475	1	29	23	1		41
Rhode Island	2,698	21	26	1,851	8	12	396	7	8	174	3		22
New York	2,234	7	18	516	21	29	1,196	20	26	1,196	8		384
New Jersey	220	15	29	1,048	14	39	1,076	11	15	458	10		458
Pennsylvania		48	60	2,987	43	70	2,291	31	74	1,595	20		1,203
Ohio		19	31	1,157	38	62	2,403	17	17	1,159	12		681
Illinois		4	6	208	1	5	78						
District of Columbia		3	8	339	11	11	1,076				10		964
Maryland		2	2	61									
Michigan		1	3	55							5		114
Wisconsin		1	6	14									
Minnesota		3	7	206									
Kentucky		1	1	24									
Elsewhere					22		951	11		589	2		60
Total	21,619	310	454	27,984	278	479	16,993	170	290	9,673	101		6,670

It will be noticed that at the height of its prosperity in the winter of 1875-6 there were reported to the National Council 27,984 members in three hundred and ten councils. If the same average of ninety to a council held true of the unreported councils, the entire membership must have been over 40,000. Of those reported, three-fourths were in New England and forty-three per cent. in Massachusetts.

Still more interesting, though far less complete, are the trade statistics. In December, 1875, one hundred and one councils reported that they had in practice some method of supplying members with goods. Of these, twenty-six councils distributed goods at cost, twenty gave dividends on purchases. The remaining fifty-four that reported had arrangements probably with ordinary private stores for reductions on the cash trade of members. The amount of capital invested in trade and owned by individual members was $30,527; the capital owned by councils as such, $5,197, of which nearly all was returned by the Springfield store. The estimated expense saved by members on account of the influence of the order in reduction of prices and dividends on purchases was fifteen per cent.

In his annual address before the National Council at Syracuse, N. Y., March 20, 1877, President Earle thus reported:

"Out of the number of councils reporting [in the United States], I have selected 94 having a membership of 7,273 that, with an average capital of $884, did a business last year of $1,089,372.55, at an average saving to the members of 14 per cent., or a profit of $152,512, equal to a saving of $21 to every man and woman belonging to those councils. If we reckon the initiation fee at $2 (and for women it is only $1, and we notice that there are 2,812 women already reported as members), and the annual dues at $2, which is a large estimate, we have the net benefit to each member above reported to be $17 for the year. It is safe to assume that the unreported sales during the past year will swell the amount [of trade] to at least $3,000,000, which at the same ratio of profit as above reported would make a saving of $420,000. Again, the returns show that the average capital of each store ($884) has been turned over once in 23 days during the whole year. Our coöperative store at Worcester, Mass., turned over its capital 25 times the past year, or once in about 12 days."

A large portion of the trade was returned as on the Rochdale plan, with capital owned by individuals, in $5 shares. A capital of $86,796 was furnished by members and $14,224 by councils, $6,800 being in Springfield. Only 41 councils were reported for 1876 as confining their trade to members. The president roundly berated the 141 councils which did not hold "public meetings or sociables," and the 184 which did not have "literary meeetings." Education was rightly deemed by the leaders to be as essential as organization.

At the next annual session at Washington, March, 1878, the reports of trade statistics were very meagre. Forty-five councils reported an aggregate trade in 1877 of $750,000. Out of the thirty-five councils reporting their capital employed, which amounted to $58,000, thirty-two councils reported their capital as owned by individual members and only three as owned by the councils. Thirty-two stores sold to everybody and confined their trade, which with two exceptions was restricted to "club orders" to Sovereigns only. Next to Springfield, the ten Sovereign stores doing the largest business in 1877, and all organized on the Rochdale plan, were the following—

Location of Store.	Capital.	Trade.
Natick, Mass.,	$2,300	$58,000
Clinton, "	3,600	40,000
Webster, "	2,200	38,000
Greenfield, Mass.,	2,200	38,000

Location of Store.	Capital.	Trade.
Kingston, Mass.,	6,000	33,000
Worcester, "	1,300	28,000
Berwick, Me.,	2,500	30,000
Utica, N. Y.,	2,000	26,000
Birdsboro, Penn.,	2,400	25,000
Akron, O.,	1,600	25,000

Of the above seven in New England, three—at Webster, Kingston and Worcester—survive. I am not informed relative to other sections. These ten stores in 1877, with an average capital of $2,630, (all furnished by individual members in $5 shares), averaged a business of $34,000; *i. e.*, they turned over their capital thirteen times a year.

Like many another association, this of the Sovereigns had grown too fast and been joined by too many ignorant, discordant elements to bear the shock of adversity. The severe and long-continued hard times, from 1874 to 1879, began to tell upon the order. Members unable to get work could not pay cash, and either left the association or induced local councils to grant them credit. Although not fully recognized at the time, this cause is now held by the old leaders of the movement to have caused the downfall of the national organization in 1879–80. The finances were crippled even in 1876, and the members of the local councils were so indisposed to assist in propagandism that the per capita tax to the National Council was reduced from twenty to sixteen cents. Receipts in 1876 fell off thirty per cent., and the services of the able lecturer, John Orvis, now of Jamaica Plains, who had organized scores of councils in New England and the West, were reluctantly dispensed with. The salary of the president was reduced from $2,000 to $1,200, and afterward to little more than living expenses during the days spent in actual service.

Though unanimously re-elected in 1878, President Earle could not longer serve. His strength was exhausted. His patient service had revealed the sincerity of his declaration of the year before, "To me it is a Christian work in which we can conscientiously ask heaven to bless us. Have we the spirit of organization, the resolution to meet difficulties, the courage of self-control, through which alone great movements are made and great reforms are led? Strong convictions precede great actions. He who believes is strong; he who doubts is weak. Clear, deep, living convictions rule the world. The only faith which really saves is that which induces us to save others."

Mr. John Sheddon, of Pennsylvania, succeeded Mr. Earle, but turned his attention more to politics and less to coöperation. But, probably, the dissolution of the order in 1879 would have been inevitable under any guidance. The failure of the national organization did not involve that of the stores, some of which still exist and will soon be considered. The same business depression, however, and lack of intelligent understanding of the benefits and conditions of coöperation, which ruined the national and state organizations, caused the failure of a large number of stores. More than half ceased to be coöperative, but it must be borne in mind that, in many of those that suspended, there was no financial failure. The very prosperity of many of the stores led to the purchase of the stock by a few and a gradual transformation into the ordinary private company.

The reasons of actual financial failure were thus summarized by President Earle in his last annual address, 1878: "Our stores have not failed from any inherent defect in our plan, but because of the injudicious manner in which it was put in practice, or to the treachery of those who tried to turn to their private advantage a project they had originally professed to support." At the last annual meeting of the National Council at Newark, N. J., March, 1879, a committee assigned similar reasons. The incapacity and dishonesty of managers, which they mention, was a natural result of the ignorance among the members and their committees of oversight of the conditions of success, and a result also of the novelty in this country of such experiments, which made it exceedingly difficult to obtain trained managers. It will be noticed that all these are difficulties which time and education may remove, and which they have already in considerable measure done, as will be seen by the account now to be given of existing coöperative stores.

IV.

EXISTING COÖPERATIVE STORES.[1]

RIVERSIDE COÖPERATIVE ASSOCIATION OF MAYNARD.

This enterprise was begun at Maynard, Mass., a village of 2,700 population, in December, 1875, by the formation of a council of the Sovereigns of Industry, the impulse being the high prices of the necessaries of life. The various systems of coöperation were adopted in turn by this company, and in the

---

[1] The assistance of Mr. Michael Twomey, clerk of the county, in the preparation of this sketch, is gratefully acknowledged.

order of time in which they have been seen to be
prominent in the rest of New England.   Members of
the council obtained goods at a reduction from the
regular retail dealers on presentation of cards of membership.   Then members clubbed together and ordered
goods from Boston, where they could buy cheaper by
retail than at home.   Each person sent a list of what he
wanted.   Goods arrived in town marked for the different parties, and were delivered by team on payment of the cost.   This not proving satisfactory,
some 30 members subscribed $105 as a fund to start
a store.   Besides this the income from the fees and
dues of members were added, and a store was
started.   Goods were sold at cost.   The officers of
the council attended to the distribution two evenings
in the week without pay.   Goods sold thus were fifty
per cent. or more less in price, Mr. Twomey claims,
than goods retailed by the other stores.   Business
increased in consequence of an increase of members
of the council desirous of getting cheap goods.   The
store had to be kept open every evening, and a man
was hired to tend it.   This cautious management,
which only incurred expense when business actually
demanded it, was one secret of success.   Soon the
growth of the trade necessitated the opening of the
store all day.   But there was no system as regards
capital or shares, those who subscribed not caring
whether they lost or not.   No interest was given, but
a small profit accrued and was divided on the capital.   There being a lack of capital for the business,
it was proposed to pay seven per cent. interest as an
inducement to get money.   This had the desired
effect in due time.   In 1878 the council seceded from
the State Council of the Sovereigns, and put its finan-

cial status on a firmer basis. The association was
reorganized and chartered under the laws of the
state, with a paid up capital of $1,500 divided into
300 shares. No one could buy goods heretofore but
members. Now it was opened to the public.

The present capital is $5,000, which the associa-
tion has just voted to increase to $10,000. The
loan capital, June 30, 1886, was $10,760.56, on which,
of course, the market rate of interest is paid. Shares
are $5 each, and one may at present hold from one to
sixty shares. The number of stockholders is 260 and
rapidly increasing. Six per cent. is allowed on capital. A yearly depreciation of two per cent. on real
estate and ten per cent. on fixed stock is allowed.
Ten per cent. of the net profits goes to the surplus
until that shall amount to thirty per cent. of the
capital. The balance of the profits is divided among
stockholders according to their trade. Anybody may
join the association on recommendation of the board
of directors, by depositing one dollar towards a share
of stock. This secures his dividend on trade, which
is retained by the association until the share is paid
for. All the employés, six in number, have to be
shareholders. They are paid a fixed salary and discharged by the directors if inefficient. The present
manager had previous experience in managing
business.

Some of the regulations governing the action of
the directors and the managers, if adopted more
generally in coöperative undertakings, would increase the chances of success:

"They (the directors) shall meet once in every two weeks at least,
and oftener, if necessary. They shall have the power of removing
the clerk and treasurer for malfeasance in office, or for other good
cause. On or before the fifteenth of each month they shall make a

statement of the receipts and expenses of the association for the
previous month, and a correct copy of the same shall be hung in
a conspicuous place in the store for the inspection and information
of the members."

In these quarterly reports the attendence of each
director at all these meetings is noted.

"The board of directors shall appoint a manager to conduct the
business of the association, subject in all things to their direction
and control. They may grant him such authority for the use of
the money of the association for the purchase and sale of goods as
in their opinion the interests of the association demand, and they
may enlarge, reduce or cancel such authority at any time. They
shall require said manager to keep a correct account of all his receipts and expenditures of money of the association and of all business of said association transacted by him or under his direction.
They shall make, or cause to be made, a thorough examination of
said manager's books at least once a month, and see that the association is in no way wronged by him. They shall also hire such
number of helpers for said manager as in their opinion may be required for the prompt transaction of the business of the association.
They shall fix the salaries of said manager and his helpers, and
shall have power to discharge or suspend them at any time. They
shall also require said manager and helpers, who must be stockholders of the association, to give good and sufficient bonds, acceptable to said board, for the faithful performance of their trusts.
They shall cause the manager to turn over his surplus money to the
treasurer at least twice a week."

Orders are taken and goods delivered, two horses
being employed for the purpose. No secrecy is
necessary. Still, few of the customers know the
cost of the goods.

Very little trusting is done, unless to accommo-
date for a few days. The greatest drawback is that
the association put up a large building costing
$15,000, the income from which is not sufficient to
meet the interest, insurance and other expenses,
thereby taking a large part of the profits which
would otherwise go to dividends on trade and help
increase the business. Goods are now sold at a reas-
onable margin of profit, and prices are the same to

all. The fifteenth semi-annual report for the six months ending June 30, 1886, is a model of its kind. The sales were $18,231.26, a gain of $2,031.23 over the preceding half year. As this increase continues, the next year's trade will be about $43,000. About one-ninth of the sales are dry goods and the rest groceries. Besides adding $73.02 to the surplus, which now amounts to $916.83, a dividend of three per cent. on purchases was declared. The lesson conveyed in the following words of one of the directors and officers of the association is noteworthy:

"In our town is a woolen mill employing 1,000 hands, which commenced paying weekly wages on the first of May, and the sales at our store have steadily increased every month since. Previously it was monthly pay, and all the other stores trusted and charged higher prices than we did. Consequently, when people could handle their pay oftener, they went where they could get cheaper and better goods, which is the cause of our increase. During the ten years of our existence we have saved over $10,000 for our members. . . . . We were strongly opposed by the other storekeepers for a long time, and they tried to boycott and slander us all they could, but now finding themselves on the verge of ruin, with their trade almost all gone, they have nothing to say."

THE NEW BEDFORD COÖPERATIVE ASSOCIATION.

Very similar is this association for the sale of groceries and provisions in New Bedford, Mass. First came a dividing store, where goods previously ordered and purchased in bulk at wholesale prices were divided among the members at cost. Then came a union with the Sovereigns, with a reorganization and charter, January, 1876. The amount of capital has been $3,000, in shares of $10 each, though much less at the beginning. The present number of owners of the 300 shares is 94. In August, 1886, it was voted to increase the capital to $10,000, with a view to buying or building a suitable store. More than half this new capital has already (December, 1886), been subscribed, and the number of stockholders is thereby largely increased. No one person can hold more than 50 shares. Interest is paid on share-capital at the rate of seven per cent. a year. Business is growing, and last year (1885-6) amounted to $48,000. A dividend of nine per cent. was paid on purchases. Prices to all are the same. All profits after deducting general expenses, depreciation and interest on share capital. have been divided equally on the purchases of all. Hereafter non-members will only receive one-half as much per cent. dividend on their purchases as do members. Any purchaser wishing to become a member and to receive the full amount of dividend on his purchases, can do so on payment of one dollar on account for a share, and by subscribing not less than one dollar a quarter, or allowing the dividend to remain until one share of $10 is paid for. Special effort is made to have all shareholders trade in the association. As most of the customers are working people, and receive their pay weekly, one week's credit is given.

The secretary, Wm. Reynolds, writes:

"For the whole ten years we have been in existence we have lost, I think, about $600; five-sixths of that amount was lost in the first six years. Up to within three years and a-half we suffered a good deal through changing of managers. The present manager took charge three years and a-half ago, and has given good satisfaction. He is a member who feels as much interested in the prosperity of the association as he does for matter of wages."

THE COÖPERATIVE STORE COMPANY OF SILVER LAKE.

It may be interesting to notice the method of coöperation and its success in a small place. Coöperation at the small village of Silver Lake, in the town of Kingston, Mass., was begun under the

auspices of the Sovereigns of Industry, June 14,
1875, and incorporated in May, 1877. The poor
quality and the high prices of many articles of food
at the time were among the causes impelling to this
attempt. The enterprise was started in a sparsely
populated locality with a meagre capital of $460,
which has since grown to $1,800, owned by 40 stock-
holders in 360 shares of $5 each. There is also a re-
serve fund of $800, the limit required by law. The
annual sales of late have been about $10,500. The
manager, who has held the position from the start,
and has had previous business experience, buys for
the store and has a general oversight of the business. Besides him there is emyloyed only a sales-
man, or storekeeper. There have been three different storekeepers in eleven years, and only one
had any previous knowledge of the business. Experience, however, was not so important where the
manager made all the important purchases. At
first only shareholders participated in the profits,
but any one could become such when able to purchase a share, if approved by the directors and
elected with less than three negative votes by the
stockholders. Now all profits, after payment of six
per cent. interest, are divided among all the patrons,
whether members or not, according to their trade.
Three thousand two hundred dollars have been thus
distributed. This dividend for the six months
ending October 1, 1886, was small, being only two
per cent. on trade, but will hereafter be more, as no
more is required for the sinking fund. The entire
expense last year on a trade of $10,385.01 was but
$470.37, or 4.7 per cent. Goods warranted of good
quality are sold at market prices for cash. No

secrecy in the management of the business is deemed necessary. A printed report is made semi-annually.

The manager, Henry B. Maglathlin, to whom I am indebted for the above, writes: "The greatest drawback is the want of a coöperative sentiment in the community, and the poverty of the people, which does not allow their trading at a cash store." In the constitution, and in the last report, occur these important words: "A true coöperator has three qualities—good sense, good temper and good will. Good sense to dispose him to make the most of his means; good temper to enable him to associate with others, and good will to incline him to serve them and be at trouble to serve them, and go on serving them, whether they are grateful or not in return, caring only that he does good, and finding it a sufficient reward to see that others are benefited through his unthanked exertions."

DANVERS COÖPERATIVE UNION SOCIETY.

One of the oldest, as well as one of the most successful, coöperative companies in New England, is the Danvers Coöperative Union Society, which was started in 1865 in the shoe-town of Danvers, Mass., on the principal of the old union stores, viz.: sales at cost to stockholders. Until July, 1869, there were no sales to outsiders. At that time the general features of the Rochdale plan were adopted, although advantage was not taken of the Massachusetts laws of incorporation, to be hereafter described, until January 24, 1880.

The capital, as incorporated, is $5,000 in $10 shares, thus distributed among 98 stockholders:

29 own 1 share each.			2 own 8 shares each.			
14 " 2 shares "			7 " 10 " "			
11 " 3 " "			1 " 13 " "			
7 " 4 " "			2 " 15 " "			
10 " 5 " "			1 " 17 " "			
3 " 6 " "			7 " 20 " "			
4 " 7 " "						

98 " 500 "

No one can hold more than 20 shares. A share is always found for one desiring it. Six per cent. interest is paid on stock. After proper deductions for depreciation are made, ten per cent. of the net profits go with the surplus fund and the rest is given to stockholders in proportion to their trade. These dividends have averaged twelve per cent. in the last six years, never running below nine nor exceeding fourteen per cent. The store trusts, though this is acknowledged to be a bad feature. Some losses result, but the temptation to long credit is removed by a provision of the constitution depriving stockholders of interest for the month if their accounts are not settled as soon as the month expires. All the trade of stockholders, whether for cash or not, is recorded by the storekeeper in his own books and on the small pass-books of the customers, that dividends on trade may be fairly divided. The trade of the 98 stockholders is about three-fourths of the whole. While sales of stock must be through the company, anyone is privileged to purchase. The trade last year was $25,000. It has been more in value, when prices were higher, but never more in bulk. The building which contains the store is owned by the association, and the financial condition is excellent. One delivery wagon is used. Sales are

at market prices, and as the non-stockholder gets no
dividends on his purchases and may not care to own
a share, other grocery stores seem to flourish in the
town. The present manager, Mr. C. H. Giles, was
appointed in January, 1886, but was previously an
assistant in the store for eight years. Five directors
audit the accounts, which are open to the examination of all. While waiting in the store for the manager one evening in September, I fell into conversation with one of the directors, who had been interested in the store since its foundation, 21 years ago,
and who became very enthusiastic over the possi-
bility of learning something of similar enterprises
elsewhere, and of having the success of this store
made public for the first time. As many other
coöperators have remarked during this investigation,
he considered the greatest need of coöperative enterprises to be a better knowledge of the location,
methods and success of each.

THE WEBSTER COÖPERATIVE ASSOCIATION.

The most interesting survival of the Sovereigns is
at the manufacturing town of Webster, Worcester
county, Mass. Here Artizan Council No. 95, of the
Order of Sovereigns of Industry, formed December
15, 1874, still retains its organization, and holds its
meetings every Tuesday evening, for social relaxa-
tion and for study of coöperative methods, with
almost, if not quite, as much devotion to the cause as
if the national and state organizations of this once
flourishing order were not six years ago things of
the past. The old initiation fee of $2 for males and
$1 for females, and annual dues of $1.40, are still col-
lected for the use of the council of 330 members, all
5

of whom own, as a condition of membership, one or more of the 860 five-dollar shares which constitute the $4,300 capital of the store. Groceries, meal, crockery and wooden-ware are sold. Applicants for membership must be approved by an investigation committee of three, and receive less than three adverse votes on secret ballot by the council. At first the council obtained reduced rates from local merchants, but in 1876 started the store. The number of shares any one can hold is limited to fifty, but, as just noticed, the stock is widely diffused. It can only be owned by members of the council. The trade has grown steadily from $46,976 in 1881 to $55,920 in 1885, and, judging from the first ten months, will reach $66,000 in 1886. Goods are sold for cash only and at market rates. After payment of seven per cent. as interest on capital, the remaining net profits are given to the 330 members of the council, according to their trade. The trade of outsiders (about one-fifth of the entire trade), is welcomed, but no special inducement is extended save, perhaps, the probability of greater freedom from adulteration than at other places. Last year a dividend on trade was declared of $3,750, being a return of nine per cent. on the trade of the council. The first manager was inexperienced and unsuccessful. The remaining two were experienced and successful. The third and present manager, Mr. Joseph Arnold, who was chosen on the death of his predecessor, "has had twenty years experience," writes Mr. J. Reilly, one of the directors, "hence the success of the last three years."

LOWELL COÖPERATIVE ASSOCIATION.

This most flourishing company, organized in 1876,

at Lowell, was also an outgrowth of the Sovereigns
of Industry. It has gradually increased its capital
from $1,000 to $10,000, which in $5 shares is now
held by 500 members. No one can hold more than
20 shares. The trade for the first six months of 1886,
according to the secretary, Mr. D. Willman, was,
groceries, $21,211, coal, $4,000. After deducting ten
per cent. of the profits for the sinking fund, which
is now nineteen per cent. of the capital, and after
paying six per cent. interest on the capital, $893.40
was paid to full members, being a six per cent. dividend on their purchases, and $24.03 to members who
were not full shareholders, as a four and a-half per
cent. dividend on the purchases made by them; for any
person on payment of twenty-five cents, if approved
by the board of managers, may have placed to his
credit three-fourths of the per cent. paid to full
members on their checks. When it amounts to a
share, a certificate of stock is issued. Non-members,
whose purchases are about one-third of the whole,
receive no share in the division of profits.

When a member dies the value of his shares is
paid to the heirs. By one provision of the constitution, which has scarcely been modified since its
adoption under the auspices of the Sovereigns, no
intoxicating liquors are to be bought or sold by the
association. The manager and nine employés are
paid a regular weekly wage. The manager had no
previous experience, but the success of the business
seems to indicate that a good choice was made.
Goods are sold at market prices. Some trusting is
done. The officers state: "We find it an evil and
are doing our utmost to abolish it."

THE SOVEREIGNS' COÖPERATIVE ASSOCIATION OF WORCESTER, MASS.

This store, started by the Sovereigns in 1875, with a capital of $1,500, in $5 shares, has increased it to $2,500, distributed among 115 persons. The trade in groceries is from $25,000 to $30,000 yearly. Five per cent. interest is paid on stock. One-tenth of the net profit is reserved as a surplus, and the rest is divided *pro rata* on trade, giving one-half as much per cent. to the trade of non-members as to that of stock-holders. This dividend has ranged from one-and-one-half to seven per cent., but averaged six per cent., which it has been for the last two years. The manager, who had had four and one-half year's previous experience, has held his present position since the store was opened.

THE PROGRESSIVE COÖPERATIVE ASSOCIATION OF WORCESTER.

Almost opposite the building of the Sovereigns' Coöperative Association is that of the Progressive Coöperative Association. In fact, in this home of President Earle, of the Sovereigns, there are to-day five prosperous coöperative stores, two being conducted by and for the Swedes of the city, with an increasing trade from year to year. The Progressive Coöperative Association, started in May, 1883, with $525, in $5 shares, has now a capital of $4,000 in the hands of 99 persons. The sales in 1884 were $23,000; in 1885, $37,000. After paying five per cent. interest on capital, and reserving somewhat for other purposes, the rest of the profit is divided among stockholders *pro rata* on their trade. A ten

per cent. dividend was thus given in 1885, and a
dividend of about fifteen per cent. will be declared
in January, 1887. Goods, it is claimed, are sold a
little under regular prices. One man with a large
trade took a $10 share and left all dividends and
interest, as many do, in the store, and January 1,
1886, after two years and four months, it amounted
to $118.43. A dozen at that time had received over
$50 on a $10, or in some cases $5 investment. When-
ever the directors desire to increase the number of
stockholders without increasing the stock, they may,
after thirty days' notice, enforce the withdrawal of
the excess over 20 shares owned by any stockholder.

A most successful coöperative store is the

PLYMOUTH ROCK COÖPERATIVE COMPANY,
at Plymouth, Mass., which commenced business
March 10, 1877, with a capital of $3,375 in $15 shares.
For the first three or four years profits were added to
capital, which is now more than $4,000. For the
past six years eight per cent. dividends have been
paid to stockholders, and all the rest of the profits
has gone to patrons in the form of dividends on their
trade, without regard to whether they owned stock
or not. A dividend of six per cent. on trade, which
now amounts to $42,000, is usual.

CONNECTICUT STORES.

There are coöperative stores at Torrington, Birm-
ingham and New Britain, Ct. THE TORRINGTON STORE,
with a yearly business of $6,000, has a novel method
of dividing profits. After paying seven per cent. on
the $8,000 capital, the per cent. borne by the profits
to the total trade is determined, but that part which
might thus go to those not financially interested in

the store is not paid them, but put into the surplus
fund, which now amounts to $3,500.   The financial
supporters of the store who receive dividends on purchases are of two classes—stockholders and patrons.
A patron is one who has paid $2 to the company.
He has no vote among the stockholders, but has an
equal percentage of dividend on his trade.   His $2
fee goes into the surplus funds.   This company began
as a branch of the Sovereigns in 1874, and was organized as a store in 1875 with $1,000 capital.   This
was increased as above in 1881, when the store organized under the joint stock laws of Connecticut.
No one can hold more than 12 shares.   The secretary,
Mr. Herman W. Huke, writes that the dividends on
purchases to stockholders and patrons has averaged
five and-a-half per cent., payable semi-annually, for
the four years ending Jannary 1, 1887.   The company never has changed the manager.   Trade, except in very rare cases, is all cash.

THE SOVEREIGN TRADING ASSOCIATION at Birming-
ham, Ct., has a yearly trade of $15,000 and a capital
of $1,050, besides a surplus. The par value of a share
is about $10.50; "the inventory value is $55 and
no share for sale," writes the president, Mr. W.
V. Bowman.   The 84 shares are in the hands of as
many stockholders.   Goods are sold at a low price to
all for cash.   No dividends are given, even to stockholders, but they receive ten per cent. discount on all
purchases.   These discounts often exceed in one
year the entire par value of the stock.

THE SOVEREIGNS' TRADING COMPANY, dealers in
groceries and meats, at New Britain, Ct., with a trade
of about $75,000, declares no regular dividends on

the 200 shares held by its 200 members. Ten per
cent. dividends are paid on purchases to members,
and five per cent. to non-members. On recommendation of the board of directors and the vote of a majority of the members, a dividend may be paid on the
stock. Seventeen dollars and fifty cents a share was
thus paid in 1885, but this was unusual. The regular
guaranteed dividends on purchases is found to be
sufficient inducement to the ownership of stock.
Membership, which is limited to 200, is always full.
Business was begun on this plan in 1876 with $250
capital. The inventory in July, 1886, revealed assets
of $12,700. The president, John B. Dyson, writes:
"Our trade is increasing. We opened up in August
last (1886), a coal and wood yard. Our store is reck-
oned among the leading stores in the city. Our
prices are used and quoted by other dealers, so that
we virtually set the prices."

ACUSHNET COÖPERATIVE ASSOCIATION.

This company, located at New Bedford, Mass., I
have not, unfortunately, been able to visit, but the
treasurer, Mr. Sylvanus Bennett, has given me a few
facts about this interesting enterprise. Beginning
in September, 1859, and therefore third in age of the
coöperative stores in New England, it has gradually
gained in strength until now it has a capital of
$6,875 in $25 shares, owned by 107 shareholders.
There is also a surplus amounting to $5,288. During
the last seven years, beginning with 1880, the dividends on this capital have averaged 27 per cent. Since
1869 the dividends paid have amounted to $38,088.
There is no dividend on purchases. The secret of this
great success is partly the way expenses have been

kept down. With a trade of from $60,000 to $70,000 annually, no team has been run, and only $3,000 has been spent for labor. A very little trusting is done, but so carefully that only $400 has been thus lost in the past 27 years.

MAINE STORES.

At least two coöperative stores in Maine (and probably more), were started by the Sovereigns: THE LEWISTON COÖPERATIVE SOCIETY of Lewiston, and THE DEXTER COÖPERATIVE store of Dexter, Maine, which pay interest on capital and dividends on the purchases of stockholders. The Dexter store, with $4,000 capital, has paid from 4½ to 12 per cent. dividends on the trade of its 188 stockholders and reports a growing business.

THE LISBON FALLS COÖPERATIVE ASSOCIATION of Lisbon Falls, Me., organized February 16, 1885, with a present capital of $6,425, has increased its trade in groceries, boots and shoes in eighteen months from $350 a month to $2,000 a month, and has been compelled to put up a building of its own, known as the Coöperative Block. Dividends are paid on the purchases of members. Three provisions of the constitution are worthy of notice, though one or more may be found in several other coöperative stores. Credit is given to members for thirty days to the extent of four-fifths of their capital invested. In declaring dividends on trade the directors may exclude from a participation in the profits the sales of such articles as yield little or no profit to the association.

The following announcement is made to other stores:

"We wish it distinctly understood by traders and business men that it is not our intention to run down prices by excessive competition, as that would be a violation of one of the essential principles of the coöperative system, because, if excessive competition, by depreciating the price of labor's products, is right in theory, on the same principle it would be perfectly right to depreciate labor's wages.

"We take our stand in the market with the intention of doing business in competition with others, on fair and honorable terms, and shall sell at the current rate; but if dealers undertake to run us in prices, they must not find fault if unpleasant consequences should result from their coming in competition with a powerful combination of workingmen."

For the seven months ending September 15, 1886, a dividend of fifteen per cent. was paid on $8,497, the amount of the members' purchases, which was four-fifths of the whole trade.

KNIGHTS OF LABOR STORES.

In many places in New England the Knights of Labor have been organizing during 1886 coöperative stores, but they have not yet been running long enough for one to judge of their prospects of success.

THE CLINTON KNIGHTS OF LABOR COÖPERATIVE SHOE STORE belongs to the three Knights of Labor assemblies of Clinton, Mass., who put in $600 capital and opened a store the first of December. In the first four weeks $600 worth of goods were sold. Any profits will go to the local assemblies, but the peculiar feature of the store is the reduction of ten per cent. in price to all members in good standing. Whatever may be the fate of the store, the effect upon the local assemblies has been remarkable. Whereas before the opening of the store many members were backward in payment of their dues, now the 1,500 Knights are prompt in payment, that they may show their membership cards and obtain their discounts at the store.

SWEDISH STORES.

THE SWEDISH MERCANTILE COÖPERATIVE ASSOCIATION of Worcester, Mass., began December 1, 1884. It now has a capital of $2,300, in $5 shares, owned by about 96 persons. The first year no dividends were declared, but in 1886, in a less expensive, though good location, under the management of Mr. A. Johnson, a dividend of ten per cent. was paid to the stockholders. The trade was $19,000, but there is no dividend on purchases.

Older by two years than the above is the FIRST SWEDISH COÖPERATIVE COMPANY of Quinsigamond, a suburb of Worcester. A dividend is here paid on trade; the annual trade amounting to somewhat over $30,000. Six per cent. interest is paid on the $3,000 capital.

ADAMS COÖPERATIVE ASSOCIATION.

Coöperative stores on the most approved principles are constantly opening. One of the most promising is the Adams Coöperative Association, for the sale of meat, at Adams, Mass. With 300 five-dollar shares in the hands of 175 members, and a trade already of $1,200 a month, although only opened September 28, the directors, December 17, 1886, write that they find the profits for the first quarter are 18½ per cent. on the capital. After paying six per cent. interest on the capital the remainder is to be divided according to purchases—non-members receiving half as great a per cent. as members.

THE ARLINGTON COÖPERATIVE ASSOCIATION.

The last distributive association on the Rochdale plan to be described in these pages is at Lawrence, Mass. Although only the second year closed Octo-

ber 27, 1886, the success achieved well shows what
intelligent workingmen can do in this direction. The
clerk, Mr. Geo. Dewhirst, writes: "We find no difficulties in management, many of us being familiar
with the Rochdale plan. We do not rely solely upon
a professional manager," yet the present manager
was trained in England to his work. The association, whose first year's history has been well described in the Massachusetts Labor Report, issued in
March, 1886, is no longer confined to employés of
the Arlington Mills, but is open to membership from
the general public on nomination by a member and
acceptance by the board of directors. Shares are $5.
After paying five per cent. interest on capital and
ten per cent. of the net profits to the reserve fund,
which is invested in stock of the Arlington Mills,
until there is a surplus of 30 per cent., the balance is divided on trade, one-half as much going to
non-members as to members. The number of members grew from July 1 to October 1, 1886, from 308
to 351, and the paid-up capital from $4,360 to $5,755.
During this quarter the gross sales were:

On merchandise................,.....$9,637	97
" dry goods.....................	233 77
" boot and shoe account........	640 42
" fuel.........................	2,226 02
	$12,738 18

A dividend of eight per cent. to members and four
per cent. to non-members was given. The directors
in their report earnestly request members to allow
their dividends to remain to their credit, saying:
"This is one of the best and surest ways for workingmen of small means to accumulate savings."

Acting on the suggestion of Mr. Dewhirst, one of
the directors, that a copy of the balance sheet of this

corporation for the quarter ending September 30, 1886, would be of much help to would-be coöperators, it is given below:

TREASURER'S REPORT FOR QUARTER ENDING SEPTEMBER 30, 1886.

CASH.

Dr. Receipts.		Cr. Disbursements.	
Cash on hand July 1	$1,616 04	Purchases	$9,319 79
Sales	12,738 18	Salaries	599 10
262 new shares	1,310 00	Expenses	344 76
Shares made up	42 90	Fixtures	281 90
Installments received	33 60	Real estate	1,250 00
Admission fees	23 50	Interest and dividend paid	428 54
Educational fund	91 00	51 shares cancelled	255 00
		Non-members' dividend	15 72
		Cash on hand	3,360 41
	$15,855 22		$15,855 22

PROFIT AND LOSS.

Dr. Expense.			Cr.	
Salaries		$599 10	Profit on sales	$2,106 24
Interest to October first		59 66		
Taxes and insurance		26 08		
Depreciation on fixtures		56 90		
Traveling expenses	$19 76			
Gas	14 72			
Ice	36 00			
Rents	71 00			
Horse hire and keeping	120 32			
Repairs on wagon	25 27			
Printing and stationery	33 00			
Sundries	24 69			
		344 76		
Dividend to members, October 1		877 52		
Dividend to non-members		15 72		
Sinking fund		126 50		
		$2,106 24		$2,106 24

TREASURER'S REPORT FOR QUARTER ENDING SEPTEMBER 30, 1886.—Continued.

LEDGER BALANCES.

Merchandise in stock	$2,304 71	Sinking fund	$1,200 00
Dry goods in stock	161 40	Share capital, 1151 shares	5,755 00
Fuel in stock	442 55	Educational fund	91 00
Fixtures	800 00	Installment accounts	64 22
Real estate	1,250 00	Interest and dividends for previous quarters remaining uncalled for... $271 67	
Cash	3,360 41	Interest quarter ending October 1, 1886... 59 66	
		Members' dividend... 877 52	
			1,208 85
	$8,319 07		$8,319 07

Respectfully submitted,

FRANK FARR, *Treasurer.*

Examined and found correct.

GEORGE HARTLEY, *Auditor.*

In accordance with the custom begun a year ago, we tabulate below the summary of the year's business by quarters. The average capital for the year measured by the amount of interest paid equals $3,840.

QUARTERS—13 WEEKS EACH.	Total Sales.	Gross Profits.	Salaries, Expenses & Interest.	Net Profits.	Dividend Divided.	Carried to Sinking Fund.	Interest Paid on Capital.	Total Return on Capital.
Fifth	$10,543 00	$1,832 64	$1,029 17	$ 803 47	$654 05	$119 42	$39 24	$ 842 71
Sixth	11,547 74	2,140 15	1,085 12	1,055 03	830 03	225 00	43 67	1,098 70
Seventh	10,556 02	1,981 48	1,089 40	892 08	711 08	181 00	49 50	941 58
Eighth	12,738 18	2,106 24	1,086 50	1,019 74	893 24	126 50	59 66	1,079 40
Totals	$45,384 94	$8,060 51	$4,290 19	$3,770 32	$3,118 40	$651 92	$192 07	$3,962 39
Totals last year, 54 weeks	38,194 94	6,120 04	3,846 98	2,273 06	1,949 98	323 08	173 24	2,446 30
Totals for two years	$83,579 88	$14,180 55	$8,137 17	$6,043 38	$5,068 38	$975 00	$365 31	$6,408 69
Percentages for this year		17 76-100 per cent. on sales.	9 45-100 per cent. on sales.	8 31-100 per cent. on sales.	8 per cent. on members checks and 4 per cent. on non-members.	17 29-100 per cent. of net profits, besides initiation fees.	5 per cent. per annum on capital.	103 19-100 per cent. on average capital.
Percentages for last year		16 2-100 per cent. on sales.	10 7-100 per cent. on sales.	5 95-100 per cent. on sales.	6 24-100 per cent. full; 3 12-100 per cent. half.	14 26-100 per cent. net profit, besides initiation fees.	5 per cent. per annum on capital.	73 68-100 per cent. on average capital.

We would recommend our members to carefully compare this table in detail with the one given in the fourth quarterly statement. You will readily see the progressive gain. The rapid growth in membership and share capital during the past quarter is an excellent indication of future prosperity.

Number members July 1st, 1886........308 | Share capital paid up............$4,360 00
Number members October 1st, 1886.....351 | Share capital paid up............5,755 00

In accordance with permission granted your board at last quarterly meeting, we have purchased land and are now erecting coal sheds alongside the B. & M. R. R., near Manchester street. We hope this will enable us to avoid the difficulties we have heretofore found in supplying coal.

Respectfully submitted,

WM. D. HARTSHORNE, *President.*

RATIO OF EXPENSES TO TRADE.

It will be noticed that the rent is only $284 a year, the wages for a trade of $50,000 are less than $2,400, and the entire running expenses for the last quarter, including taxes, insurance and a liberal allowance of $56.90 for depreciation on fixtures, but not including interest, were only eight per cent. of the sales. All directly concerned in coöperative stores should mark this carefully, as lavish expenditure for rent, teams, numerous employés and a "stylish" appearance wrecks more coöperative enterprises than any other cause. The idea of coöperation is substance rather than shadow—the best, purest goods—not display. One of the greatest savings of coöperation comes from the fact that costly plate glass show-windows, location on a main street, employés enough to be able to wait at once on all customers in the busiest hour of the day, and teams to carry home every small article, are not necessary to attract custom. If such be necessary, the first steps in coöperation have not yet been taken. A good, clean, wholesome store, in a reasonably convenient location, and one or two teams to deliver heavy goods, are of course requisite. But where a market is already secured among those banded together in a coöperative experiment, the need of these expensive means of advertising just referred to should no longer be felt. The very essence of coöperative distribution is the dispensing with the wastes of present competitive business. I had not proceeded far in this investigation before discovering that uncalled-for expenditures for rent, wages and other items was the immediate cause of most failures among coöperative enterprises. With the object, therefore, of de-

termining the percentage which all running expenses, including rent, wages, teams, heating and
lighting, ice, water, taxes, insurance, etc., could
safely bear to trade, the accounts of 11 successful
companies were obtained. Where the store was
owned by the company, the rent which would
have to be paid for it, if in other hands, has been
included in the expenses. The results are given in
the following table:

NAME OF COMPANY.	LOCATION.	Annual Trade.	Expenses.	Percentage of Expenses to Trade.
Industrial Coöp. Asso.	New Bedford, Mass.	$44,803 11	$3,832 95	.58
Natick Protective Union.	Natick, Mass...	100,176 00	7,883 32	7.8
Beverly Coöp. Asso..	Beverly, Mass..	124,901 00	8,134 47	6.5
Sovereigns Coöp. Asso.	Worcester, Mass.	28,000 00	2,500 00[1]	9.0
Coöp. Store Co. of Silver Lake.	Silver Lake, Mass.	10,385 01	408 51	3.8
Progressive Coöp. Company.	Worcester, Mass.	38,015 00	3,061 83	8.0
Riverside Coöp. Asso. of Maynard.	Maynard, Mass.	36,000 00[1]	3,530 00[1]	9.6
Danvers Coöperative Union.	Danvers, Mass..	10,828 14[2]	806 02[2]	8.0
Plymouth Rock Coöp. Co.	Plymouth, Mass.	42,000 00	3,580 00[1]	8.5
Division 108......	Salmon Falls, N. H.	48,000 00[1]	3,840 00[1]	8.0
Lisbon Falls Coöp. Asso.	Lisbon Falls, Me.	24,000 00[1]	1,440 00	6.0
Aggregate....................		$507,108 26	$39,017 10	7.7

[1] Approximately.
[2] From June 30, 1886, to December 31, 1886.

Thus in eleven representative and successful coöperative stores, selected without regard to any favorable showing in the matter of expenses, the average
percentage of running expenses to trade is 7.7. That

is, trade is thirteen times expenses. The highest
percentage, 9.6 at Maynard, is partly due to the con-
fessedly unwise action of the company in erecting
and occupying a too expensive building. Even in
that case the trade has to be over ten times the running expenses to insure dividends to purchasers.
While preparing the above table, the writer was
invited to address a company of would-be coöperators who were about engaging to pay $500 rent and
other expenses to the amount of over $2,000 without
a probable trade of more than seven times this expenditure. Fortunately the leaders of the proposed
enterprise accepted the logic of facts and will probably begin in a more humble and at the same time
more promising way. It cannot be persistently urged
that expenses should not exceed one-twelfth of the
assured trade.

BEVERLY COÖPERATIVE ASSOCIATION.

It is sometimes held that no form of coöperation
save the Rochdale can live. We have seen conspicuous instances to the contrary, though few in number, in the survivals of the old Protective Union
stores which sold at cost. The Beverly Coöperative
Association, organized at Beverly, Mass., by the
Sovereigns in March, 1875, is another instance. This
store, which has grown from a capital of $102 to
$7,000 in $25 shares and has an annual trade of
$124,900, sells at a very little above cost to everyone
and has never tried to earn a dividend. The manager, Mr. B. Larcom, Jr., who was previously a car-
penter, seems to have been just the man for the place.
He has known how to undersell every store, even if
this necessitated selling below cost on some goods

6

and to make up any losses by higher prices on other lines of goods. By careful calculation all expenses are met, and the stock to-day commands a large premium because of the surplus of $7,445.98 which has been accumulated and invested in the business. Only one share can be owned by a person. The stockholders are chiefly American mechanics, but hundreds of others, rich and poor, trade at the store. A branch store has just been opened, meat as well as groceries are sold and the trade the past year, 1886, has been $45,000 in excess of the year before.

COLLEGE COÖPERATION.
HARVARD COÖPERATIVE SOCIETY.

This society was organized by the Harvard students in March, 1882, and has been the model of college coöperation, having been followed by the University of Michigan, Yale, and the Massachusetts Institute of Technology. All members of Harvard University, of the Society for the Collegiate Instruction of Women, or of the Episcopal Theological school, are eligible to membership on payment of a fee of $2.50 for rent, clerical expenses, etc. October 25, 1886, the membership was seven hundred and twenty. The society is governed by a president, treasurer and eight directors, appointed as follows: two from the Law School, one from each class in college and one each from the faculty and the Divinity School. The society pays the college an annual rent of $350 for rooms in Dane Hall, and sells for cash and at cost to members, books, stationery, crockery, tennis goods, and other articles of general student use. Wood and coal are delivered, and books are imported from Europe. Second-hand furniture may be sold

for the students on a small commission, and every
student, whether member or not, is invited to purchase such. Professors often coöperate with the
society by giving in advance a list of the books to be
used by their classes. The annual cash business
from March, 1882 to March 1886, averaged $20,000
and is growing, the trade for September and October, 1886, being $12,000. The manager and assist-
ants are salaried. The subscriptions that helped to
start the enterprise have been refunded. An average of five per cent. net profit is made and invested
in business. The society now has $1,650 thus in-
vested aside from the fixtures. Henceforth credit
will be given to all members who will deposit cash
or other securities and who will file an acceptable
bond, signed by two bondsmen for not less than $200.

Besides this, a large list of associated tradesmen
is given in all lines of business where members may
obtain reductions of from five to thirty per cent.
from regular prices for cash on presentation of their
membership ticket.

YALE COÖPERATIVE SOCIETY.

This society, organized February 14, 1885, is so
much like that at Harvard as to need no detailed description. The membership has grown from two
hundred and fifty to over five hundred. The trade
at the cash store is from $10,000 to $15,000 a year.
The yearly fees, recently reduced to one dollar, contribute to the running expenses, and only enough
addition is made to wholesale prices to cover the remainder of the expenses. Cash trade is also promised to tradesmen, who sign a bond of $100 to give
certain reductions to members. Tradesmen are

usually very willing and eager to do this. From trade with these associated tradesmen, two hundred and fifteen students reported an average saving in 5.7 months of 1885–6 of $10.89, while the savings in this way and at the store ranged from $25 to $75. Not only in the matter of selling goods at almost wholesale prices, but in various other ways, such as delivery of college papers and periodicals, publishing notices, checking baggage, furnishing free telephone connections, etc., is the association of great benefit to the college. At New Haven an association of citizens was organized in imitation of that at Yale, and for cash obtains similar privileges.

The M. I. T. Coöperative Society.

In April, 1886, the students of the Massachusetts Institute of Technology organized a coöperative society, with twenty-five cents annual dues, which now embraces six hundred students, or more than three-fourths of the entire number. No store has yet been opened. The members obtain discounts as at Harvard and Yale from associated tradesmen. In all these cases the names of the traders' are printed and the discounts given, but some care is taken not to publish it abroad in the community, and thus arouse the unfavorable comment of other customers.

The Best Form of Distributive Coöperation.

So many have asked the writer during the course of this investigation what was the best form of coöperative stores, that at the risk of repeating a little of what has gone before I venture to refer to what have been found important features. The Rochdale plan is to be preferred, with its dividends on pur-

chases, limited number of shares of five each in the
hands of any one person, equality of vote of all
stockholders, market prices for pure goods and ex-
clusively cash trade. Expenses should not exceed
one-twelfth of the trade. Greater percentage of
dividends of trade should be given to stockholders
than to outsiders, but any one should be entitled to
that full dividend on depositing one dollar toward a
share. The dividend, however, should not be paid
such a one, but should be added to his credit, until
in that way, and by direct payment, a five-dollar
share is paid for. By this means men are encouraged to save. Provision should be made in the by-
laws for withdrawing at face value the shares in excess of, say ten, or even three, as the directors may
see fit, that may be in the hands of the largest stockholders, the exact ones from whom stock is to be
withdrawn being decided by lot when such a measure may be necessary to provide shares for those
without any who may be desirous of purchasing.
By this means a coöperative company will not only
exert a wide influence, but will attach to itself a
much larger trade than if its stock fall into the
hands of a few. It is to be hoped that the time will
soon come here, as already in England, when the
surplus funds of the retail coöperative stores of a
state will be invested in a large wholesale store,
which shall grant dividends on its sales. As soon
as productive coöperation on the plan of profit-sharing with all employés, as soon to be described, has
gained a firm foothold, such enterprises will also
furnish places for the investment of surplus funds.
Thus the patrons of the coöperative stores may be
encouraged to allow a large part of their dividends

to remain in good investments, that shall both bring them good returns and at the same time spread the benefits of coöperation.

V.

PRODUCTIVE COÖPERATION WITHOUT DIVIDENDS TO LABOR.

Thus far only that form of coöperation has been considered which is usually known as distributive coöperation. As the simplest, most easily managed and requiring least capital, the store is among all English speaking peoples the first form of coöperative enterprise. Many varieties may exist; the advantages of the system may be confined to shareholders, albeit a large number, or opened to everyone, and the benefits may be in the form of low prices or dividends on purchases, but saving to consumers is the cardinal object of all reforms in distribution.

Productive coöperation, wherein the laborers own much of the capital and have a voice in the management, is more ambitious and if it prove capable of such expansion as its advocates claim, will contribute greatly to solve the labor problem. The importance and difficulties of productive coöperation were well described by President Earle of the Sovereigns of Industry, in his annual address in 1877, when he referred to it as "the very battle-ground on which the true principles of the grand movement are to be fought out, where the conflicting interests of capital and labor are to be equitably adjusted and, it is to be hoped, permanently settled. The conditions of coöperative production are, however, more complicated than those of distributive, and it will take time and patience to discover all the methods whereby every person engaged in a manufactory shall be induced to do his best in making himself a partner in the surplus profits. What avails the successful operations and the increasing trade of distributive societies, if the relative position of capitalist and laborer, the employer and the employed, is to remain the same, and the poor toiler is still to be satisfied with the little he can obtain in the general scramble for the wealth which his labor produces?" He advised the stores to invest funds and give their patronage to coöperative manufactories.

The Sovereigns, however, as an organization, went to pieces before the above ideas could be carried into effect.

The first coöperative productive company in New England seems to have been the Boston Tailors' Association Union, organized in 1849 with fifty dollar shares. The stockholders received interest. Those who were at the same time stockholders and workers for at least three months of that year voted on the division of the profits, as appears by the Massachusetts Labor Bureau Report of 1877. Profits were divided annually by this vote among the workmen according to the amount of labor each performed. Sales were for cash. The association thus carried on operations for a few years. Many other such companies, chiefly in the manufacture of cigars, have had a more or less prosperous existence but little trace of them remains.

SOMERSET COÖPERATIVE FOUNDRY COMPANY.

The oldest example of productive coöperation which has survived to the present is the Somerset Coöpera-

tive Foundry Company, organized at Somerset, Mass.,
October 18, 1867. It may be called a joint-stock coöperative company if such a name is admissible, since it
combines the coöperative principle of large ownership
of stock by workmen in small shares and with equal
vote in the management with the joint-stock principle of dividing profits wholly on stock. The companies of this character in Massachusetts were so
thoroughly investigated and ably described in the
report of Mr. F. H. Giddings in the Massachusetts
Labor Report of 1886 that no attempt at further
investigation of them has been made. From Mr.
Giddings' report it appears that the Somerset Foundry Company with $30,000 in $100 shares, owned by
forty-eight stockholders, has been turning out an
annual product of $75,000 and paying a dividend of
ten per cent. since 1880. The foundry had been run
at a loss in private hands until these moulders bought
it up and made it pay dividends after the first year.
Thirty of the forty-eight stockholders are employed
in the business, and such are given the preference in
hiring men. The management can discharge any
stockholder, if a poor workman, but have not been
obliged to do so. Most of the work is by the piece.
Equal wages for equal work is paid to all employés,
whether stockholders or not. To quote from the
report: "Members individually and the management, as such, declare that they are satisfied that
stock owning improves the quality and increases the
quantity of work accomplished, and that this goes
far to account for the success attained." The members are of steady, saving habits and generally
excellent character. The management, as in nearly
all coöperative enterprises considered in this work, is

in the hands of directors who choose the necessary officers,—in this case, an agent, treasurer and foreman, subject to the directors.

EAST TEMPLETON COÖPERATIVE CHAIR COMPANY.

This, the second oldest existing coöperative manufacture in the state, was organized October 19, 1872. It has a capital of $20,000, in two hundred shares, in the hands of thirty-eight persons, mostly of New England birth and descent. Fourteen of these, with ten non-shareholders, are employed by the company. The value of the product is about $50,000. Dividends of five and six per cent. are paid in prosperous years, and few losses are incurred. A large working capital of about $1,000 to every employé is considered essential. In this, as in other successful coöperative companies, there have been few changes of management.

THE STONEHAM COÖPERATIVE SHOE COMPANY.

This company, of Stoneham, Mass., where three other coöperative boot and shoe enterprises are located, was organized January 9, 1873. It now has a capital of $20,000, in eighty shares, in the hands of fifty-seven stockholders. Of these twenty-five work in the mill, and nearly forty others are employed. The stockholders are said to be of all nationalities, and to have always worked harmoniously together. The annual product is $150,000 and the dividends since 1878 have been, 17, 15, 15, 21, 20 and 6 per cent. The best workmen are employed, whether stockholders or not, but the agent can discharge none of the former without the consent of the directors. The treasurer believes that $2,000 capital

must be had for every case of shoes made for the
jobbing trade.   Insufficient capital is the ruin of
many a coöperative enterprise.

THE MIDDLESEX COÖPERATIVE BOOT AND SHOE COMPANY.

The above company located at Stoneham with a
present capital of $15,000 in sixty shares, in the hands
of forty-seven shareholders, met with many losses
soon after the start in 1875, owing to the failure of
certain debtors.   Yet the record of dividends is as
follows :

1876—9 per cent.	1880—10 per cent.
1877—An assessment of $26.85 per	1881—10 " "
share to meet losses caused	1882—20 " "
by failure of customers.	1883—25 " "
1878—5 per cent.	1884—20 " "
1879—4½ per cent.	

Twenty-five stockholders and eighteen non-stockholders are employed.   Nearly all the other twenty-
two stockholders are employed in the shoe business.
The members are Americans, Irish and French
Canadians of good character.   The treasurer remarked, "Coöperators must be of good habits, economical
and saving.   They must belong to the place and have
a permanent interest in it."

As the seven other companies investigated by Mr.
Giddings, the American Shoe Company, Athol Fur-
niture Company, Franklin Shoe Company, Kingston
Foundry Company, Leonard Foundry Company,
Middlesex Shoe Company and the Wakefield Shoe
Company, resemble those just considered, they are
grouped in the table at the close of this account.

Coöperative Granite Works of South Ryegate, Vermont.

These works have a paid in capital of $2,900 in $100 shares, owned by twenty-three shareholders. Nine of the fourteen workmen are shareholders. There is no limit to the number of shares any one can own. Profits and losses are divided on the shares. The business was started in May, 1885, under peculiar circumstances which are thus described by the secretary, J. D. Grant:

"A number of stonecutters were thrown out of employment in consequence of having organized a branch of the Granite Cutters' National Union here, and not only were they denied employment by the two firms in the granite business here at that time, but were blacklisted in Barre and other granite centers in Vermont, so that they had no alternative apparently but leave the state. A large proportion of the men were householders and had families living here, and they did not wish to go away for work while there was plenty of it at their own door. And the result was the birth of this little enterprise. But this was only the beginning of tribulation, for no sooner did the aforesaid granite contractors find that we did not intend to leave the state than they hatched a scheme to have us all arrested for conspiracy, because the National Union on learning the treatment we had received had the works of the aforesaid firms declared to be scab shops, and the natural consequence of this was that those who worked there would be held to be *scabs* by all union men. We were placed under bonds, sixteen of us, which have been reduced several times and are now $200 each, and the case is in the hands of the law to-day, and not yet settled.

"Yearly business $8,000 to $10,000. Business growing. But do not consider it beyond the experimental stage yet. There has been great difficulty in securing a center of authority, each one claiming to be his own boss. The management was at first in the hands of a superintendent, but that did not give satisfaction. It was then changed into the hands of five directors, who employ a foreman for the outdoor part of the work, and a secretary and treasurer to keep the books and accounts and take contracts and transact the general business of the company. These officers are all shareholders and are hired by the day. But the expense of running the thing seems to be too much. We started with no cash capital, members putting in their shares as a rule by labor, a certain rate per month. We have never had enough capital to run the business to good advantage, although convinced that it could be done with proper facilities. We believe coöperation is the missing link between capital and labor, and no matter how many experiments may fail, the ultimate result will be success."

A few other productive companies, mostly of recent origin, with this mingling of the joint stock and coöperative principles, exist in New England, such as the Coöperative Granite Works at Quincy, Mass., the Haverhill (Mass.) *Laborer* and the printing business connected therewith, the Rhode Island Coöperative Printing and Publishing Company of Providence, with a business of $6,000 a month and rapidly growing, and the

South Norwalk, (Ct.,) Coöperative Hat Company.

The latter was organized in January, 1885, as the result of a lockout. By the conditions of incorporation the capital is not to exceed $9,000 in one hundred dollar shares, more than half of which had been raised at the time of my visit to the factory in September, 1886. No one can own more than three shares. The stockholders, mostly Americans, numbered thirty-five and in most cases worked in the business, although the management may discharge anyone for cause. The number employed is from ninety to one hundred in the busy season. Success had been good and the business was said to be growing rapidly, due in part to the patronage voluntarily given hats with the coöperative label by members of labor organizations. The manager, however, Mr. Edmund H. Bush, who was previously a workman, is a capable man, and seems entirely devoted to making the business a success. The bookkeeper remarked: "Every book is open to every

shareholder. Some feel themselves a little above
everybody else, but no great trouble has been experienced." When the by-laws were adopted it was
wisely provided that no dividend should be declared
the first year. The company was burned out at the
start and again February 22, and in part March 8,
1886, due to causes which it is thought have now
been removed. In spite of these losses the company
appears confident of success, and when visited were
making two hundred dozen felt hats of the Derby
style weekly.

In the same town of South Norwalk, Ct., was
another coöperative hat company organized about
the time of the other, but which ceased to do business in October, 1886. The president ascribes the
chief cause of failure to the refusal of the company
to pay enough to secure a good manager. He writes:
"If a man can conduct a factory he can command
high wages in any form, and a coöperative or any
other firm will have to pay them. What we ought
to have done, and what I wanted, was to get an experienced man for a manager and pay him the same
wages that any other firm would pay. I could not
carry my point with the board. I think there is
where we missed it."

At North Dighton, Mass., the NORTH DIGHTON
COÖPERATIVE STOVE COMPANY began July, 1886, with
$11,500 capital in the hands of twenty-seven stock-
holders, of which seventeen work in the factory with
five non-stockholders. Lack of capital is the greatest drawback reported. It is too soon yet to present
any results.

The following productive coöperative companies
have been chartered this year, 1886, and have in

some cases nearly completed buildings and prepared
for soon beginning business. All divide profits
wholly among stockholders, none of whom have
more than one vote in the management. The companies are:

The Scituate Coöperative Shoe Company, of Scituate, Mass., with $10,000 capital in $10 shares. All
the officers and probably all the employés will be
Knights of Labor.

The Westboro Factory Association, of Westboro,
Mass., for making boots and shoes. The capital will
be $12,000 in $100 shares.

The Agawam Coöperative Shoe Company of Danvers, Mass., with $5,000 capital in $5 shares.

North Dighton Coöperative Stove Company, at
Taunton, Mass., with an authorized capital of $11,500
in $100 shares.

The Knights of Labor Coöperative Boot and Shoe
Company, of Beverly, Mass., with $3,000 capital in
$10 shares,

The Brockton Coöperative Boot and Shoe Company of Brockton, Mass., with a capital of $10,000 in
$200 shares.

Coöperative Creameries.

In many parts of New England, Massachusetts especially, are coöperative creameries, which, like some of
the companies already described, have certain joint
stock and certain coöperative features. A description
of one or two of these creameries will suffice: The
Springfield Coöperative Creamery, organized a little over two years and a-half ago, has now a paid in
capital of $22,000 in twenty dollar shares, part of which
is invested in a fine brick building constructed for the
uses of the creamery. No one can own more than

fifty shares, or have more than one share for each cow and eight-quart can of milk furnished daily to the association. There are eighty three shareholders among the farmers within nine miles of the city. As in every coöperative enterprise chartered under state law, ten per cent. of the profits go to a reserve fund until that shall amount to thirty per cent of the capital. Ten per cent. is reserved for losses and depreciation of plant, and the rest, not to exceed five per cent., goes to the stockholders. If the business admits of it, any further profits go to the farmers in the form of higher prices for their milk. In 1884–5 the stockholders received five per cent.; in 1885–6 one per cent. About half of the milk and cream is sold and the rest made into butter. Eggs are also bought and sold. Two and three-quarters and three cents a quart is paid for milk. The great reason for starting the creamery was to furnish a steady market to the farmers for their milk. Previously, irresponsible milkmen would run in debt to the farmers, and failing, entail heavy losses upon them. There was naturally great opposition to the creamery by these old milkmen. The creamery had to buy out nineteen old routes at high rates and hire the old milkmen to sell for the new company. They depreciated the milk, however, expecting soon to buy their old routes back. Customers kept dropping off, until last February, 1886, when the creamery overcame these difficulties, and has gradually increased its trade ever since.

At Lowell, a coöperative creamery, with a capital of $25,000 in twenty dollar shares, was organized in October, 1885, to furnish a regular market for the farmers' milk. Previously, when the milk was not

sold in Lowell, it was left on the farmers' hands to
spoil. In remedying such difficulties as these the
creameries in all parts of the state seem to confer
their greatest benefit rather than in any considerable
profits to the shareholders. A very successful creamery seems to be that at Amherst, Mass., where, with
a capital of $2,700 in ten dollar shares, in the hands
of sixty-five shareholders, the annual product of butter has grown from $19,250 in 1883, when it was or-
ganized, to $29,600 in 1884, $46,225 in 1885, and about
$60,000 in 1886. Six per cent. interest is paid on
stock. In many cases, as at Springfield and Conway,
patrons of the creamery get all benefits after payment of a certain interest on capital. Creameries
are located at Hatfield, Westboro, Lee, Hinsdale,
Cummington, Conway, Egremont and Rutland, Massachusetts, and in other New England states. Most
of them are of a very recent origin. The supply of
milk is generally not large enough to permit of
great growth, but there is every indication that these
creameries serve a useful purpose and will prosper.

VI.

PRODUCTIVE COÖPERATION WITH DIVIDENDS TO LABOR.

In all cases of productive coöperation thus far considered, as in all coöperative stores, there have been
found no dividends to labor as such. No share of
the profits has gone to the workmen in proportion to
their wages. We have now to consider a development of the coöperative idea to cover this more com-
prehensive form of profit-sharing. A coöperative
company was chartered at Orange in 1879, with
$5,000 capital, for the manufacture of furniture. Ten

per cent. was reserved yearly as a surplus fund, and the rest of the profits went to the workmen in proportion to their pay. Not even interest was paid on capital, but as all the shares save three or four were owned by the employés little trouble resulted from that. Jealousies, however, arose over the pay of the men, some claiming that others were receiving too much. This led to the dissolution of the company in three years. There was no financial failure, for those who put in $100 stock received in the three years as dividends on labor, and at the settlement as their share of the property, $197, and all others received proportionally large returns.

Lynn Knights of Labor Coöperative Boot and Shoe Company.

The Knights or Labor leaders in Massachusetts are planning a great forward movement in coöperative production. Within a year several important enterprises have been started by them. The Boot and Shoe Company of Lynn, under the able management of Mr. Richard Nagle, until his resignation recently Master Workman of District No. 77, of the Knights of Labor, deserves description. In November, 1885, a few interested in the project visited Stoneham and concluded to adopt a different system from that of the coöperative shoe companies, thereby giving labor a direct share in the profits. Returning to Lynn they solicited those who promised to be congenial spirits, putting the shares at $100 to prevent too large an influx of unsuitable members. There was great difficulty in securing shareholders at this figure but $5,000 was at last secured, and the company started in April, 1886. Three weeks of that month

7

were spent in putting in machinery. A rent of $75 a month had to be paid although no business was done. A market must be made and the leaders looked forward to the July meeting of the stockholders with much trepidation. To their surprise it was then found that in ten weeks they had made $10,000 worth of goods and were $200 ahead. The capital is now, January, 1887, $9,000 in the hands of about sixty persons. Ten shares is the limit anyone can own. There was previously a small coöperative store at Peabody, near Lynn, whose agents came to the Lynn company for shoes to avoid buying prison-made shoes, and at once made arrangements to become a branch of the Lynn Company. The shares of the Peabody store were $5. The stock was raised to $2,500 and for every twenty shares one holder was selected to exchange the stock for stock in the Lynn Company, so that the Peabody store serves as a branch. A constantly growing patronage is secured among the Knights of Labor and also among other classes in all parts of New England, for a good shoe is made. Profits are to be thus divided: Ten per cent. goes to the sinking fund; five per cent. interest is paid on the capital stock; ten per cent. of the remainder goes to the Knights of Labor Assembly for a coöperative fund to be used in assisting other coöperative enterprises; forty-five per cent. is to go to capital and forty-five per cent. to labor, in proportion to wages. All the workmen must be Knights of Labor. Over forty are employed, nearly all being stockholders. Shareholders have the preference in securing work, but may be discharged for cause. Workmen who are not shareholders are encouraged to deposit at any time toward a share. The limit of the capital, according to the charter, is $10,000 and could all be raised at once, but the balance is reserved for employés. The full amount will, however, soon be used. All the workmen are beginning to own stock. On visiting the works in September, 1886, I found every appearance of success, and learned as one indication of the spirit and sincerity of the manager that he had been offered $1,200 salary by the directors, but refused to take more than $1,000. At the first annual meeting, January 3, 1887, after less than eight months operations, it appeared that, after making very liberal allowance for all possible losses, the net profits were $1,000 on a capital which at first was only $4,000, and which did not reach $8,000 until October. Business for the last three months of 1886 averaged $5,000 a month. The operatives claim that besides their share in the profits they receive the highest scale of wages in Lynn. Naturally they are very well pleased and unanimously re-elected their old manager and directors. Mr. Nagle writes: "We are perfectly satisfied with the results. The secret of success is by applying business principles, such as keeping down expenses, etc." Some, it is to be hoped not many, of the other shoe manufacturers in Lynn are said to be bitterly opposed to this factory, since their employés, seeing the brilliant success of the coöperative company and learning the exact profit made on every shoe, demand for themselves a greater share of the product. One wholesale dealer in leather refuses to sell even for cash to the coöperative company, but the members of the latter are too well pleased with their success and too confident of the future to be easily daunted.

SPENCER COÖPERATIVE BOOT AND SHOE COMPANY.

At Spencer, Mass., is a similar company started April 12, 1886. At first it was poorly managed and attempted to occupy a large and expensive building. About the first of October, 1886, it elected Mr. James H. Kelly manager and removed to commodious but less expensive quarters, with most happy results. Although the mistake of the first few months have prevented any dividends, the last few weeks of 1886 witnessed a profitable business, and there seems now good reason to expect success from the enterprise. The capital of $6,200 in $10 shares is in the hands of about one hundred persons, although five own nearly half the stock. As the company is incorporated under the laws of Vermont, instead of Massachusetts, there is no limit to the amount of stock anyone may own. This is a serious mistake, and should be remedied, or a few or even one may ultimately control the entire business. Although only fifteen workmen are employed the monthly product is about $2,500. The work being on a finer quality of shoes than elsewhere in Spencer, skilled workmen had to be imported from other parts of New England. All employés and stockholders must be Knights of Labor. Only two of the fifteen as yet own stock. Despite this, all the workmen are deeply interested in the success of the business, because, as at Lynn, they receive a share of the net profits. The plan of profit-sharing seems a model one and resembles that of Mr. Batterson in his Rhode Island Granite Works elsewhere described. After payment of six per cent. interest on capital and a deduction of twenty per cent. for a sinking fund, the body of employés receive such a part of the net profits as their combined yearly wages bear to the capital. Each workman will receive profits according to his wages.

Goods are bought and sold for cash or very short credits. An agent is traveling for this company, as is another for the Lynn company, and business is increasing. The agents visit the Knights of Labor assemblies and in many cases induce the members to call at the local stores for the shoes with the label of the coöperative company and thus create a market. Where coöperative stores sell boots and shoes, as at the Industrial of New Bedford, Mass., the Knights of Labor Coöperative Shoe Store of Clinton, Mass., and the Coöperative Shoe Store of New Market, N. H., a market for the products of the factories is secured. The agents sell somewhat outside of New England, in New York and adjacent states.

The Coöperative Printing and Publishing Company of Boston.

Mr. George E. McNeil, the veteran advocate of coöperation and champion of labor, organized, in the summer of 1886, a printing and publishing company in Boston on the same general principles as the Coöperative Boot and Shoe Company of Lynn. Only six per cent. interest is to be allowed on stock. Of the rest of the profits ten per cent. is laid aside as a reserve fund, twenty-five per cent. is to go to contingencies, for possible losses or for increase of business, ten per cent. goes to labor, five per cent. to District 30, K. of L., and the other fifty per cent. is to be devoted to propaganda. Every employé must own stock and must belong to the Knights of Labor and to the Printers' Union. The capital is 500 shares of ten dollars each. The limit of shares any one can own is fifty. There were in September, 1886,. twenty-five employés and about forty shareholders. The excellent composition and electrotyping of *The Labor Movement* edited by Mr. McNeil, is the work of this company. In a recent conversation he said his company was meeting with very good success and had all the orders it could fill. Four causes may be assigned for this success; the personal influence of the manager, good management, the quality of the work done, and in connection with this, and as one factor also in securing patronage, the coöperative enthusiasm which this scheme has aroused among the workmen and the friends of coöperation. It is of course too early yet to predict what permanent success will attend the enterprise. The outlook is certainly encouraging.

The Coöperative Iron Foundry Company of Nashua, N. H.

This company, employing fifty hands and doing an annual business of over $40,000, is thus described in a recent letter by one of the officers:

"This Coöperative Foundry Company was first organized 27th January, 1881, with a capital of only $4,000. Shortly afterwards it was increased to $8,000, then again to $16,000, and finally last summer the capital stock was increased to $22,000. This last increase was made to furnish tenements or homes for some of the help. Necessity was the cause of the starting of this venture—the help were refused their honest wages, an attempt to cheat them was frustrated through the firmness of the men, who put three attachments on the property, and after one year of law suit succeeded in getting their wages, and finally came in possession of the foundry and plant. The workmen were assisted by friends or outside parties, who helped in buying stock and now own some of it. Our stock has always sold at a premium as high as $115 on $100. From $115 to $109 has been the range. Any money made over six per cent. will be divided next May among the workingmen, stockholders and non-stockholders. Both will be treated alike as far as wages and profits are concerned, except dividend on stock.

"All must comply with the rules and regulations. Business is carried on as any fairly conducted stock company should be, no useless salaries paid to ornamental officers; every man must earn what he gets. While we have carried some men still we manage to get along without much friction. The competition in the market is very great. We know that some concerns make work at a loss, consequently *burst;* other concerns get the cheapest help they can find, and do everything to undersell others. Underselling is the ruin of the workingman; fair prices and fair wages should be the motto of all.

"I cannot close this communication without stating that in the commencement of our undertaking a squad of Boston moulders were imported into New Hampshire to take the places of the men who were endeavoring to obtain their lawful wages and by lawful means, but after a few days in the foundry they were compelled by the sheriff to go out, and they went. We have our foundry lighted by electric light; we believe we have the only foundry in New England lighted by electric light."

The National Knights of Labor Coöperative Elastic Fabric Company of Chelsea, Mass.

This company for the manufacture of suspender web, goring web for congress shoes, elastic web for gloves, etc., has paid for twenty thousand feet of land at fifteen cents a foot, erected and paid for a building one hundred by forty-six feet and put in part of the machinery, so that the company expects to begin business early in 1887 with about twenty-five employés, men and women. The capital stock is $5,000 at five dollars a share, no one being allowed to hold over one hundred shares. The by-laws are in accordance with the Massachusetts law of incorporation soon to be described. After payment of eight per cent. interest on the capital and ten per cent. of the net profits to the reserve fund, one-third of the remaining profits are to go to labor,

one-third to capital and one-third to the coöperative
fund of the general and district assemblies of the
Knights of Labor. A portion of the wages of every
workman will be reserved until he possesses a five
dollar share and every employé will probably have to
be a member of the Knights of Labor. The difficulties already overcome have been so great that the
courage of the founders has been well tested. The
enterprise originated in a strike of the girls of Martin
Bros., of Chelsea, who, it is claimed, had cut down
their pay. This and subsequent labor difficulties
have cost the workers of the place $14,000 in a few
months, and have greatly hindered the raising of capital for the new company, though increasing the
motives for it and stimulating the zeal of many.
One thousand dollars of the four thousand two
hundred dollars paid in capital in September was
held by local assemblies of the Knights of Labor,
which had contributed twenty-five dollars and up-
ward apiece. Only Knights of Labor are permitted
to own the stock. A considerable market will be
secured among the labor organizations of New England. After enumerating some of the difficulties thus
far experienced, one of the management, Mr. Leonard M. Small writes: "But we will get there before
long and have already a number of customers ready
to take our goods."

VII.

COÖPERATIVE BANKS.

The objects and general benefits of coöperative
banks, or, as they are often called, coöperative building and loan associations, have been so well described
by Dr. Albert Shaw, in his account of coöperation

in Minneapolis and St. Paul, that it only remains
for me to give the peculiar features with a little of
the history and statistics of the banks in New
England.

Inasmuch as Massachusetts has the only general
law on the subject in New England, and includes all
but five or six of the entire number, about fifty in
this section, the present state law under which all
these banks must be organized deserves some study.
The late Hon. Josiah Quincy[1] was chiefly instrumental in securing the main provision of the present law[2]
in 1877. Some of the important features of the Massachusetts coöperative banks are the following: The
capital of a coöperative bank is limited to $1,000,000
in shares whose full value is $200 each. The shares
are not paid for at once, or within a short time of
commencing business, as is usual with corporations,
but are paid at the rate of one dollar a month until
paid for, a new series of shares being issued semi-
annually and annually. This would require two
hundred months, or sixteen and two-third years, for
the payment of a share, but for another feature of
the system. The money accruing to the treasury
from these monthly payments, and from all other
sources, is loaned every month to such of the shareholders as offer the highest premium. The profits
from these loans and premiums furnish the dividends,
which usually amount to between six and seven per
cent. Every one can borrow for aid in building or

---

[1] See interesting and clear presentation by J. Q. A. Brackett, of
the present system in *The State*, October 3, 1886, and reprinted by
T. O. Metcalf & Co., printers, 48 Olivet street, Boston, Mass., 1886.

[2] The text of the present law, as amended to date, is to be had in
convenient form of Mr. D. Eldredge, 36 Bromfield street, Boston,
Mass.

buying a home, to the amount of the par value of his share, but no more. As security he must offer his shares and such other property as may appear to the directors sufficient. They will lend up to the full market value of such security, while the savings banks are only allowed to lend to the extent of sixty per cent. of the assessed value of the real estate security.

It may be asked, how a poor man who has not real estate can borrow, even of a coöperative bank? The answer made by Mr. Brackett, and confirmed by others, is that ·· if he wishes to buy an estate he can borrow of the bank the greater part of the needed purchase-money, and give as security therefor a mortgage of the property at the same time he receives his deed therefor. Of course the bank cannot furnish the whole amount of the purchase-money.'' But if one has a very little money and will subscribe to, say five shares, he can borrow $1,000. A man can thus build a house, mortgaging it as security to the coöperative bank. The would-be borrowers, as has been said, bid for the privilege. Premiums range from nothing to fifty cents a share, but rarely over twenty-five cents for any length of time. The by-laws of coöperative banks usually require the successful bidder for a loan to pay for one month's interest and premium immediately. If a loan is not approved, a month's interest and premium are forfeited. Successful bidders can always obtain shares for their loan. If one borrow $2,000 at twenty-five cents premium a share he is subject to three monthly charges—first, a payment of ten dollars on his ten shares, which he had first to take before borrowing; secondly, a payment of $2.50, as a premium, and thirdly, a payment for interest, which, on $2,000, at six per cent. (the usual rate) is $10. In .all, then, our friend pays $22.50 a month, until his shares mature in about twelve years, when the bank will hold his note for $2,000, and he will hold shares worth $2,000. The two accounts are cancelled, and thus for a little more than the expense of rent in the meantime a man finds himself owner of a comfortable home.

Anyone with sufficient security, which, be it observed, most workmen have not, might borrow the $2,000 of a savings bank, pay five per cent. interest, or $1,200 during the twelve years, and then pay the debt, making $3,200. The same sum borrowed of a coöperative bank will involve a payment during the one hundred and forty-four months, at $22.50 a month, of $3,250, besides the loss of, perhaps; $400 more in compound interest to the close of the twelve years on these payments. Two things are to be said: First, it is very unusual for one to pay a twenty-five cent premium for a very long time. Whenever he finds it possible to bid off $2,000 for a lower premium, say ten cents, he may do so, and with this loan pay off his other, borrowed at a higher rate, for one can repay his loan at any time, retaining his shares or not, as he chooses. The only charges are that the borrower must pay double interest and premium for one month, and have a new mortgage made and the old one discharged. Even this reduction will not fully equalize the payments in the case of the borrower from the the coöperative and from the savings bank. It, therefore, remains to say that, human nature being as it is, scarcely one man in a thousand will make provision

by constant voluntary monthly deposits in a savings
bank to repay his $2,000 mortgage at the end of the
twelve years. This is the real justification for the
existence of the coöperative banks. Their shareholders feel compelled to make their regular monthly
payments. Before the man is aware of it, he has
paid for his home and acquired the valuable habit of
saving. The results are in every sense satisfactory,
seven per cent. dividends being made.

Again, these banks enable the depositors, who are
in most cases wage earners, to use their own deposits, whereas the money deposited in the savings
banks in Massachusetts, $300,000,000 in 1886, sup-
plies the capital of the great employers of industry,
and thus does not so directly promote the coöperative
ideal,—a larger share by the workmen in the profits
of industry. In addition to nearly all the advantages
of the justly famous postal savings banks of Europe,
the coöperative banks give much higher interest and
keep the deposits for actual use among the lenders
of the immediate neighborhood. By the Massachusetts law at least twenty must be associated together
for organizing such a corporation, and no person can
hold more than twenty-five shares of the ultimate
value of two hundred dollars each in one corporation.
No member can have more than one vote. A member may at any time, on thirty days' notice, withdraw
any shares not pledged as security for loans, besides
paying any fines that may be due. He loses by so
doing such portion of the profits previously credited
to the share, and must bear such a proportion of any
unadjusted loss the by-laws may determine.

When each unpledged share matures, *i. e.*, reaches
through payments and dividends the value of two

hundred dollars, the holder is to be paid with interest at six per cent. for any time that may intervene
before the payment. All dividends on the stock
cease. To avoid any run on the bank it is provided
that at no time shall more than one-half of the funds
in the treasury be applicable to the payment of such
matured shares, without the consent of the directors.
The same provision is made with regard to those who
would withdraw their shares, as any one may on
thirty days' notice, if he is willing to forfeit such
part of the accrued profits of his share as the directors may determine. The directors make deductions
varying from nothing to one-fourth of the accrued
profits. The banks confine their loans to the State
and generally to the immediate vicinity.

Only one serious danger seems to confront these
banks, unless we accept the temptation of a borrower
to offer such high premium as forty cents for loans,
and that is that in about twelve years after the opening of the banks, there will be insufficient funds in
the treasury to pay off the shares, which then begin
to mature every six months. Assets will be sufficient
but not available, *e. g.* one of the Massachusetts banks
has two hundred and thirty-five shares, amounting to
$57,000 that will mature about January 1890, and one
hundred and seventy-two shares, amounting to
$34,400, six months later, or $91,400 that year. The
amount of dues received in 1885 was $61,044.87 and
the total cash received $95,755.03. These latter
items may increase, and judging from past growth,
will increase fully seventy per cent. by 1890; but
even then one-half of the total receipts must go to the
payment of shares. If now any considerable number
of others wish to withdraw their shares—and eight

hundred and ninety-five shares, one-sixth of the
whole number, were thus withdrawn from the bank
in question in 1885, as an ordinary incident of business,—the bank will be in a tight place. To be sure,
the directors can legally postpone payment, after paying out one-half of the cash in the treasury at any
one time, but, since in six months another series
matures, postponement could not long be indulged in
without ruin to the credit of the bank.

The law has carefully provided for this. The
directors may in their discretion and pursuant to the
by-laws, retire the unpledged shares of any series and
enforce their withdrawal at any time after four years
from their date of issue. The full value of the
accrued profits on the shares to date must be paid in
such cases, instead of part, as in the case of with-
drawals by members. The shareholders whose shares
are to be so retired shall be determined by lot under
such regulations as the directors may prescribe. By
means of this provision a bank may anticipate the
time of payment, whenever it cannot loan its funds
at satisfactory premiums, and thus be relieved of all
danger. Although the oldest banks founded in 1877
had only been running eight years in 1885, three of
them then began paying off shares of the first series.
Four hundred and ninety shares in the three banks
were thus retired that year, leaving but three hundred
and seventy-six shares in the first series and three
hundred and thirty-eight in the second.

Mr. Eldredge, who is of deserved authority on this
subject, having been instrumental in founding and
prominent in managing several of these coöperative banks, thus writes of the safety-valve just mentioned:

"It is being made use of regularly every six months, but the majority, to their discredit be it said, make no use of it whatever. The right of the directors to retire the shares (after four years) is truly a safety-valve. By a judicious use of it, unsaleable money may be used in paying off the shares, and again it is wise to redeem the old series to a size (in number of shares) which will admit of paying in cash at maturity. In two years the maturing of shares first issued will occur, and then comes the trying time with the system here. Those banks which have so reduced their series as to be able to pay cash, will ride safely along—otherwise, otherwise. Then is the time, and continuously thereafter, when the banks have got to be financiered well or go to the wall. Assets enough, probably, but not *cash* to pay indebtedness. The series are like notes becoming due, and, as the banks have no quick assets of any description, it behooves them to provide. Those banks which can sail along for a few years following the first maturity of shares, will be able probably to continue. Some banks in this state are apparently utterly ignoring, or vainly putting off, the evil day, for they have large series and do not retire any shares."

It must be said, however, that there is yet time to make such provisions as the law allows, and most banks will probably be wise enough to do so, when their attention is strongly called to the danger. If any failures occur it will not be on account of the system or the law, but of the folly of directors. Furthermore, as Mr. Eldredge remarks, the worst effects will be felt during the first year or two after the shares begin to mature, since these banks, having abundant assets, can easily arrange for the payment of shares if they will plan accordingly.

As no bank can possess over $1,000,000 actual paid-in capital, any danger of a progressive increase of liabilities and business until too large to be well-manged is out of the question.

As long ago as 1850 there were coöperative building associations in this section which reached the height of their prosperity about 1860 and failed, in some cases most disastrously, in others honorably,

about five years later. This was due to the grave
faults in the system, and this in turn to the prevailing ignorance of how to conduct such associations.
Among these defects as contrasted with the present
system may be mentioned: The old banks, instead
of issuing $200 shares every six months, payable in
one dollar monthly installments, made but one issue
on those terms. When these shares matured in
from ten to thirteen years, and were then paid back
as the law required, the bank was thereby extinguished. In the old, if one who took a share failed
to keep up his monthly payments he was fined so
heavily that his share would be entirely extinguished
in about six months. Now only a two per cent. fine
can be exacted, and this fine cannot extend beyond
six months, when, if no further payments are made,
the value of a share at date, less certain accrued
profits, is returned to the owner of the share. Nor
in the old law was there any provision for the retire-
ment of shares before their maturity at the discretion of the directors. An important fact, bearing on
the assumption of some, that the less legislation the
better, is thus presented by Mr. Eldredge: "The old
banks were not hedged about with detail legislation.
The act was a brief one, and set up a skeleton arrangement, leaving a mass of details to be arranged
by each association to suit itself. The new are
hedged about, many details being inserted in the act
—valuable ones, too."

Examples by the hundred might be cited to show
how the present system of coöperative banks has
already, in less than ten years after the passage
of the law, enabled the wage-earners, who are their
chief patrons, to own homes of their own, and in

many more cases obtain returns of six and seven per
cent. on their monthly deposits.

A few facts gleaned from the report for 1885 of
the bank commissioners of Massachusetts will tell
much of the story. There were then thirty coöperative banks, since grown to forty. These thirty had
78,565 shares in force, 11,836 members, 2,482 bor-
rowers, and $2,512,335.86 assets, an increase of
twenty-five per cent. over the preceding year. The
report for 1886 is expected to reveal a corresponding
increase for that year. At this rate a great future
may be expected for these associations. The loans
are almost entirely on real estate security, but a
small amount is loaned by each bank on the mere
security of the shares. The by-laws of the several
banks limit their loans sometimes to $2,000, some-
times to $5,000, the limit of the state law. The
smallest loans are as low as twenty dollars.

Since it is the policy of these banks to loan all
moneys in the bank once a month, or to use them to
pay off shares, and, as all the business can be done in
a small part of every day, no great expense for
vaults and clerical force is necessitated. One man
in Boston, Mr. Eldredge, is secretary of three banks—
the Pioneer, Homestead, and Workingmen's—all of
which have the same office and hold their monthly
meetings on different evenings in the same hall. In
other places the secretary can engage in other business, *e. g.:* Mr. F. W. Dickinson, secretary of the
Springfield Coöperative Bank, carries on a large
undertaking business. The entire yearly expense
for salaries of the twenty-seven banks, which had
been running a year in 1885, was only $9,686, an
average of $358.74.

8

In the summer of 1886 Maine had a coöperative bank at Richmond and another at Bangor. Rhode Island had one at Providence, and Connecticut one at New Haven. There being no general law of incorporation of such banks they were incorporated under special charter.

VIII.

GROWTH OF COÖPERATION.

LAWS GOVERNING COÖPERATION.

While the other New England states have no general law for the incorporation of coöperative companies, Massachusetts has maintained in this direction her customary lead in wise labor legislation by the law of 1866 and the subsequent amendments thereto, the most important of which were adopted in 1870 and 1879. By the present law the capital stock is limited to $100,000 and cannot be less than $1,000. No one can hold more than $1,000 or have more than one vote however many his shares. There must be an annual distribution of profits and earnings among the workmen, purchasers and stockholders, as provided in the by-laws, but ten per cent. of the net profits must first be appropriated for a contingent or sinking fund until there shall have accumulated a sum equal to thirty per cent. in excess of the capital stock. The word "coöperative" must form part of the corporate name, and shares to an amount not exceeding twenty dollars in the aggregate are exempted from attachment and execution. All incorporated companies must make full returns annually to the secretary of the important items of their business such as their nominal and paid-in capital, number of shares, and their assets and liabilities of all kinds. An abstract of these is printed with the certificates of incorporation of all other companies and is most valuable to those interested in coöperation. Of course many companies are not incorporated, but by far the larger part take advantage of the law, which gives the stockholders greater security and increases the credit of the company.

STATISTICS.

From these reports to the Massachusetts Secretary of State, some surprising facts appear. For instance it is commonly supposed that since the downfall of the Sovereigns as an organization coöperation has been practically dead in the state, whereas these reports show that there was never so much capital invested in coöperation or so much prosperity manifest as now. A few summaries which I have made from the tables given in these reports will prove this:

Distributive Coöperation.

Date.	Paid in Capital.	No. Stores Incorporated.	Average Capital.
1877	$71,279	30	$2,376
1885	92,375	27	3,421
1886[1]	124,430	30	4,181

The growth is not in the number of stores, although a great increase in that respect is probable in the immediate future, but in capital and trade, which is the surest guarantee of success. The percentage of successes to failures is much greater than ten years ago, although the exact figures cannot be given. Over ninety per cent. of business firms fail. Coöperative enterprises since 1880 in New England can show fully as good a record, indeed much better

---

[1] From returns to me of incorporated and the very few unincorporated companies.

—a fact too often overlooked by those who consider failure the sure outcome of coöperative efforts.

The summaries given above refer only to distributive coöperation. The figures for productive, coöperation exclusive of creameries, which belong entirely to the present decade, is even more encouraging. In 1875 the Secretary of State reported nine manufacturing companies with a total capital of $73,250 or an average of $8,139. In 1885 he reported ten companies with $166,900 capital, or an average of $16,690, —a growth in ten years of over one hundred per cent. This growth has continued through 1886. At least four new companies in Massachusetts began business that year, and report excellent prospects. To this must be added the thirty coöperative banks, since grown to forty, reported in 1885 with a capital of $2,512,335.86, and now nearly $1,000,000 more, none of which existed prior to 1877.

From the tables compiled with much care, which are to be found at the close of this account, it appears that productive coöperation in twenty companies in New England can boast a business of $1,000,000 a year. Coöperative stores have a trade of over $1,750,000. Coöperative creameries do a business probably of $1,000,000 and at least $3,250,000 are now invested in coöperative banks. Aside, then, from coöperative insurance companies and from the trade of probably $500,000 at liberal discount to grangers, the yearly business of the coöperative companies of New England amounts to between $6,000,000 and $7,000,000.

Our record of the early years of the coöperative movement embraced more of failure than of permanent success, although it is safe to assert that most of the so-called failures returned to the community, and very often to the supporters of the enterprise, a full equivalent of the money and time expended.

The history of the last ten years, and more particularly of the period since 1880, reveals an increasing number of successes. Mr. George E. McNeil, of Boston, recently remarked to the writer that failures were due to the fact that "the coöperators failed to coöperate." All that is now rapidly changing and the future of coöperation has seemed never so bright as to-day.

Mr. Wm. F. Young, of Wakefield, Mass., previously referred to as prominently identified with the early days of the coöperative movement in this country, writes: "The failures and mistakes of this movement, as well as of other union and coöperative efforts in this country, convince me that what is most needed to insure success is 'more thorough personal culture and education upon economic questions among the working people. I trust the work you have in hand will do much toward meeting this necessity."

THE SOCIOLOGIC SOCIETY OF AMERICA is the name taken by a society for the promotion of coöperation, which was organized in New York in 1882 by Mrs. Imogene C. Fales. An important meeting of this society for the formation of a national coöperative board was held in the parlors of James Freeman Clarke's church, Boston, September 25, 1886. At this meeting Mrs. Fales unfolded the great results of the Central Coöperative Board of the United Kingdom. Organized in 1870, this board in 1885 had a membership of six hundred and seventy-nine societies. Funds necessary for its work are obtained by a payment of 2d. per annum from each member of a society which joins the union. The board collects, and through numerous leaflets and its organ, *The Coöperative News,* distributes information about the coöperative societies of Great Britain. By these means and a yearly congress much is done to promote coöperation. A similar work was mapped out at this Boston meeting for our own country. A national coöperative board was organized to collect and diffuse information, of which Mr. Samuel Whittles, Jr., of Fall River, Mass., was elected chairman, and Mr. George Dewhirst, of Lawrence, Mass., secretary. The first number of the quarterly journal of this society, *The Coöperative News,* issued in January, 1887, with the gentlemen just named and Mr. F. H. Giddings, of Springfield, Mass., as editors, gives promise of taking up the work of coöperation where the *Bulletin* of Worcester, the old-time organ of the Sovereigns of Industry, laid it down. Although so recently established, this coöperative board, through its chairman, Mr. Whittles, was able to render material assistance in some portions of this investigation.

Mr. Geo. McNeil called a meeting of the delegates of the coöperative societies known to be located near Boston to meet in that city September 22, 1886. Although only about eight societies were there represented, a very interesting meeting was held. For the first time these societies, through their delegates, had an opportunity of comparing notes and considering the best forms of productive and distributive coöperation. It was agreed that, as in the latter, the Rochdale plan was preferable, so in the former a share in the dividends to all employés, whether stock-owners or not, as prevails in the Coöperative Publishing Company, 25 Beach street, Boston, and the Knights of Labor Coöperative Shoe Company of Lynn, was by far the best and truest form of productive coöperation. Indeed, in other places, some writers, notably Mr. Giddings, have gone so far as to urge that the state shall only recognize those manufacturing companies as coöperative which do thus share profits with all employés. This informal meeting adjourned with a resolution instructing Mr. McNeil to call a convention of all coöperative companies in New England to meet at such time and place as should seem to him best. It is to be hoped that through this source, or that of the Sociologic Society, a congress of coöperators will be called in the near future.

IX.

PROFIT-SHARING.

Profit-sharing is the term usually applied to that form of coöperation where the employés, without contributing to the capital, or having any control in the management, share in the profits aside from their regular wages. There has been long in vogue, however, in the New England fisheries a form of profit-sharing where no wages at all are paid, but the workmen rely for reward wholly upon a stipulated share in the catch. The Massachusetts Labor Report for 1886 describes the system. It appears that at Gloucester the owners furnish the vessel, provisions and fishing gear, and receive half of the gross value of the catch, after deducting a few trip expenses, such as towing, ice barrels, etc. Out of this half, the owners pay the skipper a percentage, while the crew from their half must pay the cook, the cost of the medicine and a small percentage to the widows and orphans' fund. The crew's half is divided among the men in proportion to the catch of each, if the fish have been caught with hook and line. When seines are used, as in mackerel fishing, the crew share equally. Where the crew find provisions, dories and fishing gear and pay all expenses, except hiring the skipper, as in haddock fishing, they receive three-fourths of the gross proceeds. The value of the vessels used varies from $3,000 to $12,000. The average is about $5,000. The owners are reported as saying that the wages system would be impracticable. "We should get a lot of loafers, and the business would go to ruin. It is the stimulus of profit-sharing that has made our famous skippers," while the fishermen are reported as saying : "We could not live on wages, for the active, skillful men would fare no better than the lazy; there would be no inducement to secure the largest possible catch ; the business would become unprofitable and wages too low to tempt first-class men."

The Peace Dale Manufacturing Company.

The oldest example in New England of profit-sharing of the type so common on the continent of Europe, is the Peace Dale Manufacturing Company at Peace Dale, R. I., a village of twelve hundred inhabitants, about thirty miles southwest of Providence. From the full account in the Massachusetts Labor Report and from correspondence with the treasurer, Mr. R. G. Hazard, the following facts are gathered:

This company, the oldest woolen mill in the United States, dating back to 1804, and the first to use the

power loom, is still in the hands of the Hazards of
the third and fourth generation in descent from the
founders. With a capital of about $400,000 and a
yearly business in the manufacture of shawls,
worsted coatings, cassimeres and other woolen fab-
rics of about $600,000, it employs an average of
four hundred and fifty hands. Two-thirds are English, Irish, Swedes and Germans, the majority being
Irish. Two-fifths are women. Profit-sharing began
with a circular to the employés January 1, 1878,
announcing that thereafter, for as long as the company might choose, a part of the net profits after
payment of wages, interest at a very moderate rate
on capital and a percentage for a reserve fund against
losses, should be given yearly in March to all employés
who were in the employ of the company seven
months of the year, ending February 1. This share
to labor—not far from one-half the net profits—was
to be given to each of the employés in proportion to
the wages received from the company during the
year. Very singularly, the owners who are also
managers, reserve no salary for themselves, but trust
to their dividend for reward. During the eight years
since the plan was initiated the severe depression in
the cotton business has only enabled payment of dividends during four years as follows :

January 31, 1880, 5% on wages, $5,842 40
    "   1881, 5   "   5,999 65
    "   1882, 3   "   3,760 14
    "   1883, 3   "   3,760 35

Despite the failure to pay dividends, the firm ex-
press themselves satisfied that their experiment has
been a success in preventing waste and encouraging

conscientious work, which is so important to the moral as well as the material good of the community. An increased care and diligence on the part of the employés can be seen. In a circular to the help in 1883 the principles on which all profit-sharing is based are thus stated: "Every weaver who makes a mispick, every burler who slights her work, every spinner who makes a needless knot, in short, every person who makes waste of any kind, of course makes the amount to be divided smaller by making a loss to the concern; and we think a manifest improvement is evident."

The circular for 1884, after regretting the failure to earn dividends that year, adds: "It is believed, however, that a large majority [of the employés] have been as careful and as conscientious as possible, and the officers of the company look with pride upon such, hoping and believing that the system of participation will yet produce good results, far beyond what it has accomplished in the past." The last circular, of March 1, 1886, shows the spirit of the management. Expressing great disappointment at the continued inability to pay dividends, the circular concludes: "It is with satisfaction, however, that we look upon our undisturbed condition of mutual confidence and esteem. As long as this continues we have one very important element of success. We are truly thankful that this element exists, and we trust that it will exist as long as a mill stands in Peace Dale." In a letter of October 14, 1886, the treasurer writes me relative to the general applicability of profit-sharing: "I see no reason why it should not apply to all trades using labor, outside of machinery. No use in applying it to anything purely

mechanical.   The greatest foe to success is the ignorance of the laboring men.   Intelligence must exist
to some extent in order to have any good result."

THE NEW ENGLAND GRANITE WORKS.

At Westerly, R. I., are the quarries, and at Hart-
ford, Conn., the offices of the above company, owned
by J. G. Batterson, who introduced profit-sharing
January 4, 1886, by a letter to his superintendent,
James Gourlay.   The following extracts are taken
from this, which was printed and circulated among
the men:

"DEAR SIR: In regard to the various questions which have
arisen from time to time, touching the proper relations of capital to
labor, and which at times have assumed such menacing attitudes
that we have been forced to decline orders of considerable magnitude, for the reason that we could not run the risk of a "strike,"
which might involve us in heavy loss and damages, I have determined to submit to you the following propositions, with the hope
that they may prove acceptable to the men employed by us:

"First. On all orders executed at the New England Granite
Works quarry, in Westerly, R. I., during the year 1886, commencing January 1st, *ultimo*, both capital and labor, in proportion
to the amounts or values contributed by each, shall share in the
net profits made on such orders during the year."

The capital is $250,000 with an output of $500,000.
The wage of the three hundred and fifty to five
hundred employés are, say, $200,000.   The latter
figure is merely given for illustration, and is not to
be considered official.   But if we suppose the wages
are $200,000, then, since the capital is $250,000, the
dividend to labor would be $\frac{200.000}{450.000} = \frac{4}{9}$ of the entire
net profits after one-third of the profits have been re-
served as a guarantee fund.   To this guarantee
fund are charged all losses by bad debts, or credits
for materials and labor during the year.   At the end
of the year all outstanding accounts and bills re-

ceivable are to be treated as good under the guarantee, and therefore available in determining the net profits.   If the guarantee account does not prove to be sufficient to cover the losses the amount must be made up by the stockholders, but when it is more than sufficient the surplus will belong to the stockholders.   Continuing the quotations from Mr. Batterson's letter:

"Second. The net profit shall be determined in the following manner, viz.: out of the gross receipts, or from the capital employed, shall be drawn, first, the wages of the men employed as journeymen, whether by day's work or piece-work, at the rates mutually agreed upon or otherwise established, which shall be paid monthly; second, all other expenses of conducting the business, including superintendence, traveling expenses, clerk hire, taxes, insurance, and legal interest on the capital employed, shall then be deducted and paid out of the gross profits, and the balance remaining shall be treated as the net profits, from which a dividend shall be declared and paid in manner and form as hereinafter provided.

"Third. The net profits having been determined, the entire amount shall be divided into three parts, one part to be appropriated and paid as a dividend to labor, one part to be appropriated and paid as a dividend to capital, and one-third to be reserved as a guarantee fund, to which fund shall be charged all losses or bad debts, or credits given for materials and labor during the year.

"Fourth. The labor dividend shall be made and paid before any dividend is paid to capital, and such payment shall be made at the end of each fiscal year, or as soon thereafter as the books can be written up, an inventory taken, and the net profits determined.

"Fifth. When the net profits have been determined as aforesaid, the same may be verified by a competent accountant or auditor, to be selected and agreed upon by the parties interested; and when such accountant shall certify that the net profits have been correctly and fairly determined, then the dividends may be paid; but such accountant or auditor shall not be at liberty to disclose or make public any other facts concerning the business audited than a simple verification of the accounts, and the sum total of the net profits for the year, available for the purpose of a dividend.

"Sixth. As the labor dividend is intended for labor only, no officer, superintendent, overseer, clerk, agent, or other employé drawing a salary, or however otherwise paid, nor any contractor or sub-contractor, who for their own account and profit, contract or agree for a "lump sum" to do and perform the whole or certain specific parts of the work upon a building, monument, or other structure, such work being outside of and not subject to an established or agreed bill of prices, either for day's work or piece-work, therefore no such officer, superintendent, clerk, apprentice or contractor will participate in any dividend paid to labor, as hereinbefore stated.

"Seventh. No workman who during the year shall have been discharged for good and sufficient cause, such as drunkenness, insubordination, bad workmanship, etc , or who leaves the employment of the company without the consent of the superintendent in writing, shall be entitled to participate in any dividend of profits for the year during which such discharge has taken place.

"Eighth. No workman shall be deprived of his dividend who has been discharged arbitrarily, or without good cause, or who has been discharged for the reason that the superintendent has not sufficient orders on hand to justify his further employment.

．　　　．　　　．　　　．　　　．　　　．　　　．　　　．　　　．

"Twelfth. The control of the business must necessarily be in the hands of the stockholders. Men employed every day in mechanical labor cannot watch the markets, or possess that aptitude for business management on a large scale which is requisite to success, but they can do much in stopping the leaks caused by inefficient and bad workmanship.

"Thirteenth. All work done or money earned by the employment of machinery will be counted to the credit of labor and capital alike, and the profits made thereby will be subject to the same rule for distribution as for profits otherwise made.

"Fourteenth. No officer, director, or stockholder, shall receive any salary or compensation, except for services actually rendered, and time actually spent in the service of the company, all of which shall be as fully stated, as the amount of service contributed by any other person in the employment of the company.

"Fifteenth. The rate of wages per diem, the bill of prices for piece-work, and the number of hours to constitute a day's work, shall be determined by mutual agreement on or before the first day of January in each year, and any disagreement which may arise during the year between the superintendent and workmen in regard to the same shall be settled by arbitration.

"Sixteenth. The rate of wages per diem and the bill of prices for piece-work shall not be reduced by the superintendent to affect any contract on hand, or taken upon the rate of wages or bill of prices prevailing at the time such contract was made, neither shall the rate of wages or bill of prices be advanced by the workmen to effect such contracts, and if so advanced the difference in cost by reason thereof may be adjusted in making up the dividends.

"With the results of a long experience before me, I am convinced that the payment of fixed wages to a large number of men carries with it no inspiring motive to the attainment of a high standard of excellence, either as to the quantity or quality of their productions; but, on the contrary, it tends to indifference and laziness to such an extent that the measure of a fair day's work is not that quantity which can easily be done and well done by a good man, but that quantity which an indifferent man is willing to do and can do without much effort. The consequence is that the best men who are endowed with both energy and skill, soon break away from the restraints of idleness, and by the 'bill of prices fixed for piece-work' obtain a larger freedom and a larger reward for their labor; and the fact appears also, that this system of compensating labor is most remunerative to the employer, which brings us to the point, that the average and indifferent workman does not earn his wages when tested by the standard of his own 'bill of prices.'

"I believe, then, most thoroughly in the efficacy of *individual interest* as the only available stimulant to natural ambition, and the best results both to capital and labor. When the interests of capital and labor are made identical and well balanced, I believe the conflict between them will cease, and both will be the gainers thereby.

"I sympathize with the laudable ambition of the skilled workman to emancipate himself from the thralldom of a service in which he has no other interest than daily wages, and who aspires to that identity of interest in results which begets self-respect, and a worthy pride in the success of his own company or corporation.

"When the workmen are all interested in the results of their combined labor, there will be no room for those who are unwilling to earn, and fairly earn, the wages which they demand. When the industrious and skillful workman sees that his own earnings are being diminished by the slothful and unskilled workman at his side, he will rebel, and demand, as he will have the right to do, that a better man shall be put in the place of the laggard.

"My purpose is, if possible, to secure a community of interest which shall be recognized and admitted to be fair and equitable, claiming no more for capital than is sufficient to hold it in such employment, and giving the balance to labor. Whether my propositions are practical remains to be seen."

Mr. Batterson informs me that after this first year, 1886, no profits will be paid to those who have not been in the business one year and that an increasing per cent. of profit will be paid employés according to their years of service up to five years. A few years ago there was a long strike when the men, says Mr. Batterson, kept him from hiring other employés until he took legal proceedings against them. But the bitterness of that struggle seems to have been allayed, so that even before the introduction of profit-sharing the company's relations with its employés were friendly.

The experiment has fully met the expectations of Mr. Batterson, who said in September, 1886: "There has been no year since I have been in the business when the men worked so well and took such an interest in the business as they have this year." His remarks to a reporter of one of our large dailies are thus given under date of December 31, 1886:

"We had no strikes during the year, and as the men have looked out for one another's work it has generally been done well. As they have an interest in seeing that what is done is done thoroughly, they supervise themselves to a great extent, and there is a saving in that respect. The new plan will be of more advantage to skilled than to unskilled workmen especially this year, for not long after the arrangement went into effect the laborers in the quarry heard of an advance in wages of men similarly employed in Maine, and they, too, demanded the same increase. It was granted them, but the advance, under the conditions of the agreement, will be deducted from their surplus at the end of the year.

"We have had no trouble with strikes; no trouble with contracts. We do not ask our men whether they belong to a union or not; we are more interested in whether they are capable men and thoroughly understand their work. When the profit-sharing was first proposed the men, or at least some of them, did not take kindly to the plan. But they took hold of it well after the start, and what is more, they liked it and did their best to carry it through. We hope to make a dividend, but the accounts for the year are not yet made out and the result determined, and so I can't give you any figures about the profits to be divided among the employés of the company. Our plan is an experiment, and I don't believe that anything like it has been tried in this country. I can't say how it would apply to other industries. There are some, of course, to which it would be inapplicable from the nature of things, but there are others for which it would furnish a solution for many difficulties and perplexities arising from the relations of capital and labor."

ARA CUSHMAN & COMPANY, SHOE MANUFACTURERS, AUBURN, ME.

Being unable to visit Auburn, the letter of Mr. Cushman and his address to his men on inaugurating his important plan are so good that full extracts are made. He writes under date of October 15, 1886 :

"The employés are to receive regular weekly wages at the current prices paid in other factories. The firm is to receive— 1st. Interest on all capital employed in the business. 2d. A fixed amount, as salaries to the partners for the management of the business. 3d. A fixed amount, or a percentage of what may be due from our customers at the end of each year, to guarantee against losses. 4. A percentage of the net profits for a 'Surplus Fund' until said surplus shall amount to a certain percentage of the capital used.

"After these conditions have been met, the profit remaining, if any, is to be divided between the employés and ourselves in the proportion that the annual amount of wages paid bears to the annual sales, which will be between twenty-five and thirty per cent. All of these sums and percentages have been satisfactorily fixed between the firm and the three representatives of the employés.

"We commenced under this plan April 12th last. So far affairs have progressed very satisfactorily, and in the main we are pleased with the spirit the men and women manifest, and the interest they show in the business. We have not looked for and have not given our employés reason to expect a large dividend.

"The result of the six months business just ended is such that we think there will be something to divide at the end of the year's business. Our annual sales are from $1,000,000 to $1,250,000. Number of employés, 650 to 750. Amount of our annual pay-roll, $250,000 to $275.000.

Mr. Cushman's address to his employés March 27,. 1886, and subsequently printed and distributed among them thus closes :

"This dividend shall be based on the amount paid to each employé during the year for labor. No one to be entitled to a dividend who has left the employ of the firm against its wishes, or been discharged for any reason other than sickness or want of work. The management of the business to be entirely in the hands of the firm, and to be the same as now, unless better methods can be suggested. Three of the employés are to be selected as representatives, with whom the firm will arrange the details of this plan, and who will be sufficiently informed about the conditions and results of the business to enable them, at the end of each year, to report whether the conditions agreed upon have been correctly and faithfully carried out. These representatives are not to disclose or make public any fact concerning the business except the amount or percentage of dividend available for the employés. They shall be persons in whom both the firm and the employés can place the utmost confidence. They must be citizens of Auburn, and two, at least, be owners of property and interested in the growth and prosperity of Auburn. If, with one year's trial, this system shall have worked as well as we hope, and is likely to prove practical and satisfactory, we shall, if it is the wish of many of our workmen, change the organization of our firm into a corporation, so that the capital may be represented by shares of stock. We will then set aside a limited part of the stock, or number of shares, for such of the employés to buy as would like to invest their money in that way; the stock thus owned by the employés to receive the same return in interest and dividend as that held by ourselves.

"In this proposition we now present you, we ask you to run no risks and make no guarantees; for this reason the dividend to you must be smaller than it possibly might be, if you, with us, shared the risks of the business. We intend the wages paid you weekly to be fully an equivalent to you to the amount to be set aside for capital, management, and the risks and guarantees of business. I do not wish to give you reason to expect a large dividend on the amount of wages earned; for a small percentage on the amount of our pay-roll would be a large sum. Our pay-roll last year was about $250,000—five per cent. of which would be $12,500—quite a respectable amount. But five per cent. on the earnings of one man whose pay in the year amounts to $500, is only $25, which by itself is not a large sum, but, if multiplied by the number of men and women we employ, it would amount to a sum worth working for.

9

"This also illustrates how difficult it sometimes is to advance the rate of wages. Ten per cent. advance in our prices would amount to $25,000 a year, a sum that could not always be taken from the yearly profits, except by the process of algebra, where signs are used, but it is only *twenty cents* a day to a man whose pay is $2.

"Suppose all the men and women who work for us in all the different places and capacities, should be able, in some way, to make their services worth to the business five per cent. more than they ordinarily are, that would amount to $12,500. Is it not possible that in transforming into boots and shoes ready for the foot of the wearer all the material of all the kinds we use in a year— leather of the different kinds, cloth, thread, silk, nails, wax, flour, glue, cement, twine, ink, paper, boxes; that in the process of cutting and assorting the leather, in the wear and tear, in the breaking of tools and machinery, in the use of time, and in the damage to material, in the different processes—more economy could be used, more saving made, less waste allowed and damage caused? With sufficient thoughtfulness, study and care, could not the saving in all the ways I have indicated, and in others that may suggest themselves to you, be made to amount to a sum which, if divided to all the employes, would be equal to 2½ or 5 per cent. increase in your pay? I will particularize a few of the ways in which saving might be made or losses prevented. If a man in cutting grain leather uses one foot more for a case of slippers than is absolutely necessary, the loss on his work is from fifty to sixty cents a day. Such a result might easily happen, and be hardly perceptible to a looker-on, or even to the cutter himself. If a cutter of calfskins fails to put every part of the skin where it will count for the most, or in the place to which it is best adapted, and thereby makes his shoe vamps cost a half cent a pair more than they otherwise would, the loss on his day's work amounts to at least a dollar. If a man who cuts split quarters fails to place his pattern and cut the stock so as to get the most possible from it, losing only one-eighth of a cent a pair, he fails to earn for us as much as he might by more than a dollar a day. If a man in cutting sole leather fails to adjust his die as closely as it possibly might be, and for that reason gets one less sole in every three sides of leather, the difference in the cost of the soles cut in a day would be only a small fraction of a cent on a single pair, but on his day's work it would amount to more than $1.50, which is a very large per cent. on his wages.

"In the stitching room, if the thread and silk is not all used from the spool, or if the ends are left longer than they need to be, or if twine is wasted in tying up the cases, the loss might be very

slight on a single pair of shoes, but on a day's work it would be
enough to lessen the value of the services of the woman doing the
work to some extent, and when multiplied by one hundred women
and then by three hundred days, the amount would be enough to
buy many new dresses and bonnets. If every man and woman
who runs a machine could save an unnecessary wear and prevent
all breaking by careless use, we should have to buy less machines
and 'spare parts,' and our machinists would have less to do. In
the item of damage to material and goods in the process of manufacture—tearing shoes in lasting, damaging soles in fitting, scratch-
ing or cutting uppers in stitching, and in all the different ways in
which damage happens—if this could be reduced to the least possible amount, the saving made or the loss prevented would, I doubt
not, be equal to the earnings of the smartest workman in the
factory.

"If for any reason the plan we propose should not be found to
be as satisfactory to you or to ourselves, as we hope and expect, we
shall be ready and hold ourselves at liberty to discontinue it. We
present the proposition after mature thought, with the sincere
wish and earnest hope that if accepted and understood it will be
of some pecuniary benefit to you. But we do not wish it to be
understood, as we do not claim that it is, a philanthropic or be-
nevolent project. Sound business principles make the only foundation for a permanent and successful business.

"We mean for ours to continue on such a basis, and for our
methods to be in harmony with correct thinking and just and
liberal action. We hope it will be an incentive to all to make their
services as valuable as possible, and a means of securing to all
just and full returns for what they contribute to the success of the
business. If it should prove to be a method by which capital and
labor can together achieve better results, and an element in making labor more thoughtful and considerate and intelligent, and
both capital and labor more considerate of each others' interests,
our purposes will be realized. We would be glad to see Auburn
have a larger measure of success. We would be glad to see hun-
dreds more of homes occupied and owned by workingmen. We
hope the land that has recently been sold in house lots will be cov-
ered with neat and comfortable houses, and owned by men and
women who are conducting the business and doing the work that is
making, and is to make Auburn, now the 'lovliest village of the
plain,' a large and prosperous city."

At the close of Mr. Cushman's address, remarks
were made by several of the employés in hearty

approval of the proposition, and three satisfactory representatives were selected from the employés to act with the firm in arranging and carrying out the details of the plan.

The success thus far has been stated in the above letter.

NEW HAVEN WIRE COMPANY.

The necessity for success in profit-sharing of some feeling of mutual confidence between employer and employé, based on previous fair dealing and generally peaceful relations, is emphasized by the experience of the New Haven Wire Company. This company [presided over by Mr. E. S. Wheeler, of New Haven, presented to their employés a well-devised plan of profit-sharing January 1, 1886, in accordance with which, after deduction of six per cent. on capital and a "proper sum for betterments and repairs to the works," one-fourth of the net profits should go to labor, but it met with no response from the men and was not therefore adopted, although in Europe employers have often persisted in their profit-sharing and waited, until the actual payment of dividends at the end of the year converted their employés. Mr. S. A. Galpin, treasurer, writes:

"It might, perhaps, meet with a more cordial reception from our men if again offered to them, because it is not improbable that their feelings in regard to it were very materially influenced by the fact that they had been for the preceding six months engaged in a strike, which closed by their surrender within a few days after this circular [of January 1, 1886,] was issued."

GEORGE H. KINGMAN.

Mr. George H. Kingman, a large shoe manufacturer at Brockton, has taken in his workmen as members of his firm. He is said to make a written agree-

ment with each workman by which the latter agrees
to contribute any stated sum he may think best to
the capital stock of the business. Upon this sum
Mr. Kingman agrees to pay a stated percentage per
year from the profits of the business, while person-
ally assuming all risk of possible loss.   Any workman
may leave work on thirty days' notice, taking with
him the money invested in the business.   The men
may belong to any labor organization, but being
members of the firm they are not to strike or be
locked out.   Mr. Kingman writes: "The workmen
agree that a fixed per cent. on what money they put
in shall represent their share of the profit.   I also
have the right to employ or discharge whomsoever
I choose.   The plan has worked perfectly thus far,
and I see no reason why it will not be satisfactory
to all concerned."

Profit-Sharing in the Gas Manufacture.

Mr. Eliot Tette, of 11 Walnut street, Boston, introduced profit-sharing in the early part of 1886 among
the employés of several large gas corporations in
which he was interested.   In a letter of October 18,
of that year, he thus describes his plan:

"My general plan in regard to profit-sharing in the companies
which I have charge of is to promise to the men a certain percentage on the semi-annual dividend, this percentage being divided
equally among the men.   For instance, if the business of the company has been such for six months as to warrant a dividend of
3 per cent, I have divided among the men 3 per cent. on the total
amount of dividend paid to the stockholders.   If through want of
care on the part of the men accidents have happened, or there has
been waste of material or any other neglect through which the
amount of *net* earnings has been diminished (and with them the
dividend also) so that only 2½ or 2 per cent. can be paid, the men
get a sum of money equal to 2½ or 2 per cent. on the amount of the
dividend—and if for any cause it is necessary to pass a dividend

the men get nothing. The plan has been appreciated by the men, who show, I think, more than ordinary interest in the success of the companies. I think well of the plan thus far, and propose to extend its application to other corporations in which I am interested."

It will be noticed that a three per cent. dividend on a capital of $20,000 would be $6,000, and three per cent. of that only $180. It must be borne in mind, however, that capital in the gaslight business bears an unusually large ratio to labor. On being asked if each man could expect to receive enough of the profits, under his mode of division, to be much affected thereby, Mr. Tette replied : "If anybody wants to carry out any plan of profit-sharing, he must of course make the amount divided among the employés sufficiently large to be acceptable to them. This is what I have done, and the men have expressed to me their gratitude and their appreciation of the plan."

BOSTON HERALD.

January 1, 1887, the Boston *Herald* instituted profit-sharing among their three hundred and twenty employés, including compositors, reporters, editors, counting-room, delivery and stereotype departments; in fact every one except space writers, who are paid by the piece for articles.   Their circular is as follows:

TO THE HERALD'S EMPLOYÉS :

We beg to tender our New Year's greeting by stating to you a purpose which we have had for some time under consideration, and which we believe will be of interest to you.

We have decided to give our regular employés this year, as an experiment, a portion of the net profits of the business, after we have reserved a fair rate of interest on the capital invested.

The portion of the profits to be given to the employés will be divided among those who shall have been in the regular employ of the firm for the whole year, and they will share in proportion to wages received. The amount to be divided will depend upon the financial results of the business, and we ask all our employés to coöperate with us in making these results as favorable as possible. We hope this experiment may be so successful that profit-sharing may be adopted by us as a permanent policy.

In addition to this division of profits, we suggest that a Herald Benefit Society be established, to which every employé shall contribute a small sum each week, and to this sum we propose to contribute a sum equal to the gross amount contributed by the employés.

The object of this society would be to provide a weekly allowance during sickness or disability, a fixed amount to be paid to some person designated in case of death, and possibly some form of pension for those who for any proper cause are unable to continue their work. We suggest that the details of the business and benefits of this society be managed by an executive committee, which should include representatives of the various departments of the business and ourselves.

We request that one person may be designated by each department to meet with us at an early day, for the purpose of discussing and arranging the rules to govern this benefit fund.

With the compliments of the season, we remain,

Yours truly,

R. M. PULSIFER & CO.

Mr. Pulsifer writes January 17 : "The idea has been received with pleasure by our men."

The idea of profit-sharing is rapidly gaining ground in New England, and many manufacturers are only waiting to see the results of present experiments before adopting similar measures themselves.

It is stated that the Sperry Manufacturing Company of Ansonia, Conn., manufacturers of carriage hardware, divided a share of their profits with their employés at the last annual meeting.

As this goes to press news comes of the announcement made January 15th, by Rice & Griffin, manufacturers of mouldings, sashes and blinds, to their seventy-five employés, that in addition to regular wages one-half of the net profits of the business,

after reserving six per cent. interest on capital, will
be given at the end of the year to all employés who
have been in the business over six months of the
year, according to their wages for the year. As the
net earnings of the company have often been twelve
to fifteen per cent. on the capital, there is here
promise of a generous return to labor. As some one
remarks: "There is not likely to be any strike in the
Rice & Griffin Company this year."

Intimations are rife of still other experiments,
which really need be called experiments no longer.
Whether all admit the wisdom of profit-sharing or
not, this much can be said : With one or two exceptions, noteworthy chiefly as exceptions, not a failure
of the experiment can be found in this country or
Europe, and even in the two or three cases where for
reasons not wholly the fault of men the plan was
finally abandoned, there was no failure of the company that tried the plan. In other words, while
coöperation has risks incident to all business, indeed
has had greater risks in the past, though promising
better results in the future, profit-sharing, even if a
failure, brings no failure to the business, and has
every prospect of being a grand success directly from
both a material and moral point of view. The proportion of profits to go to labor must vary with the
nature of the business, but the principle of giving
some part seems destined to a wide application in the
immediate future.

X.

STATISTICAL TABLES.

The claim of exhaustiveness is not made for the following tables. Some companies, probably, have been overlooked. But the attempt has been made to include all large coöperative companies and as many smaller ones as possible. No company has been included which does not give an equal vote to all stockholders, without regard to the number of shares owned by them:

DISTRIBUTIVE COÖPERATION.

NAME.	Location.	Date of organization.	Capital.	Number of shares.	Number of shareholders.	Annual Trade.	Method of dividing profits, goods being sold at market prices, unless otherwise specified.
New Bedford Indust'l Coöp. Asso	New Bedford, Mass.	1876	$3,000	300	94	$48,000	Equal per ct. dividends on purchases of all.[1]
Coöp. Store Co. of Silver Lake	Silver Lake, Kingston, Mass.	1875	1,800	360	40	10,500	" " " " "
Plymouth Rock Coöp. Store	Plymouth, Mass.	1877	4,000	225		42,000	" " " " "
Sovereigns Coöp. Ass	Worcester, Mass.	1875	1,500	300	115	28,000	One-half as much dividend on trade to non-members as to members.
Adams Coop. Asso	Adams, Mass.	1886	1,500	300	175		Same as last.
Arlington Coöp. Asso	Lawrence, Mass.	1884	5,755	1,151	351	50,000	
New Britain Coöp. Store	New Britain, Conn.	1876	12,700	200	200	75,000	10 per cent. div. on purchases of members. 1/5 " " non "
Danvers Coöp. Union Society	Danvers, Mass.	1865	5,000	500	499	25,000	Dividend on purchases of members.
First Swedish Coöp. Store Co. of Quinsigamond	Quinsigamond, Worcester, Mass.	1882	3,000			30,000[2]	" " " " "
Gardner Sovereigns Coöp. Asso	Gardner, Mass.	1875	3,600	1,000	260	36,000	" " " " "
Riverside Coöp. Asso of Maynard	Maynard, Mass.	1874	5,000[3]	860	330	66,000	" " " " "
Sovereigns Coöp Asso of Webster	Webster, Mass.	1876	4,300	2,000	500	50,000	" " " " "
Lowell Coöp. Asso	Lowell, Mass.	1876	10,000	800	99	37,000	" " " " "
Progressive Coöp. Asso	Worcester, Mass.	1883	4,000			24,000	Dividends on purchases of members.
Lisbon Falls Coöp. Asso	Lisbon Falls, Me.	1885					" " " " "
Lewiston Coöp. Society	Lewiston, Me.						" " " " "
Dexter Coöp. Store	Dexter, Me.		4,000		188		
Grange Store of Lebanon	Lebanon, Conn.					16,000	Dividends on trade of all stockholders and patrons who pay $2.
Birmingham Coöp. Store	Birmingham, Conn.		1,050	84	84	15,000	10 per cent. on purchases of members.
Beverly Coöp. Asso	Beverly, Mass.	1875	7,000	280	720	124,901	No dividends on stock or trade. Sell at cost.
Harvard Coöp Society	Cambridge, Mass.	1882			500	20,000	" " " " "
Yale Coöp. Society	New Haven, Conn.	1885				13,000	" " " " "
Division 108	Salmon Falls, N. H.	1850	6,986	341	202	48,000	6 per cent, interest on capital. Low prices to everyone.
Natick Protective Union	Natick, Mass.	1866	6,000	575	600	100,000	Same as last.
Coöp. Store of Rochester	Rochester, N. H.	1876	7,000	32		40,000	" " " " "
Carrol Coöp. Asso	Carrol, Me.					4,000	Benefit of low prices confined to Patrons of Husbandry.
Norway Coöp. Trade Asso	Norway, Me.	1877				6,000	Same as above.

Name	Location	Year	Capital	No.	No.	Business	Remarks
Foxcraft Coöp. Asso.	Foxcraft, Me.	...	...	...	...	4,000	Benefit of low prices confined to Patrons of Husbandry.
Belmont Coöp. Asso.	Belmont, Me.	...	...	...	...	4,000	" " "
Patrons Coöp. Corporation	Portland, Me.	1877	40,000	8,000	...	175,000	Benefit of low prices confined to Patrons of Husbandry; to trade, dividends.
Torrington Coöp. Store	Torrington, Ct.	1874	8,000	320	...	60,000	Same as above.
Torrington Grange Store	Torrington, Ct.	1879	...	...	...	16,000	" "
Samoln " "	Samoln, Me.	...	...	...	...	...	" "
Morrill " "	Morrill Me.	...	...	...	...	...	" "
South Paris " "	South Paris, Me.	...	...	...	...	...	" "
Norway " "	Norway, Me.	...	...	...	...	...	" "
Topham " "	Topham, Me.	...	...	...	...	...	" "
West Bath " "	West Bath, Me.	...	...	...	...	...	" "
Freedonia " "	Freedonia, Me.	...	...	...	...	...	" "
Dixmont " "	Dixmont, Me.	1884	2,300	460	96	19,000	Benefit in way of dividends on stock, and low prices confined to members.
Swedish Mercantile Coöp. Asso.	Worcester, Mass.	...	...	...	...	...	Same as above.
Old Spain Coöp. Society	Weymouth, Mass.	1882	1,500	300	130	30,000	" "
Division 42	Worcester, Mass.	1847	18,000	130	130	150,000	" "
Amherst Coöp. Asso.	Amherst, Mass.	1859	1,200	275	107	42,000	" "
Acushnet " "	New Bedford, Mass.	1871	6,875	50	50	65,000	" "
Danvers " "	Danvers, Mass	1886	2,500	600	...	36,000	
Brockton Coöp. Cash Store	Brockton, Mass.	1886	3,000	200	...	...	
Coöp. Market of Webster	Webster, Mass	1886	1,000	200	...	...	
K. of L. Coöp. Store Asso.	N. Brookfield, Mass.	...	1,000	...	...	...	
Industrial Coöp. Asso.	Olneysville, R. I.	...	...	...	...	...	
Union Coöperative	Lowell	...	...	...	...	...	
Canadienne de Lowell	Massachusetts	...	5,000	...	...	...	
Central Union Asso.	New Bedford, Mass.	...	...	...	...	...	
Aggregates as far as reported—53 companies			$187,666	19,813	5,470	$1,609,401	

¹Lately increased to nearly $10,000. Per cent. of dividends on purchases to non-members henceforth will be only one-half that to members.

²Unofficial.

³Lately increased to nearly $10,000.

The trade reported by the thirty-three stores making returns is $1,609,401· The twenty-five stores giving returns also of capital reported a trade of $1,508,401 on an aggregate capital of $118,466, that is, capital was "turned over" 12.7 times. Applying this ratio to the seven other stores that reported their capital, amounting to $19,100, but not their trade, and we may estimate their probable sales as $242,570. If, now, we suppose twelve stores making no returns did an average business of $4,003 or $48,036 in all, we find the entire trade of the fifty-three stores to be $1,900,007 made up as follows:

Trade of thirty-three stores reporting $1,609,401

Probable trade of eight others whose
    capital is $19,100   .   .   .   242,570

Probable trade of twelve others   .   48,036
                                           ——————

                                      $1,900,007

In view of stores necessarily overlooked in this incomplete survey, and in view of the increase of trade of the other stores since returns were received, it is safe to estimate the entire business of coöperative distribution in New England at $2,000,000.

PRODUCTIVE COÖPERATION.

The following table is taken from facts and tables given in the Massachusetts Labor Bureau Report of 1886, giving the figures of 1885.

NAME.	Location in all Cases in Massachusetts.	Date of organization.	Annual Product.	Capital.	Number of shares.	Number of shareholders.	Stockholders employed.	Employees not stockholders.	Average dividends.
American Coöp. Shoe Company	Stoneham	1882	$50,000	$30,000	120	91	22	23	...
Athol Coöp. Furniture Company	Athol	1879	15,000	5,000	50	33	8	3	...
East Templeton Coöp. Chair Co.	East Templeton	1872	45,000	20,000	200	38	14	9	1.83¹
Franklin Coöp. Shoe Co.	Stoneham	1883	50,000	20,000	40	69	26	10	...
Kingston Coöp. Foundry Co.	Kingston	1876	20,000	11,900	119	56	11	9	0.75
Leonard " "	Taunton	1877	75,000	25,000	250	51	40	10	3.62
Middlesex Coöp. Shoe Co.	Stoneham	1875	90,000	15,000	40	47	24	18	10.35
Somerset Coöp. Foundry Co.	Somerset	1887	75,000	30,000	300	48	30	10	7.60
Stoneham Coöp. Shoe Co.	Stoneham	1873	150,000	20,000	8(?)	57	25	35	14.15
Wakefield Coöp. Shoe Company	Wakefield	1883	55,000	15,000	150	80	12	8	8.
Aggregate—10 companies			$605,000	$166,900	1,379	570	212	135	

¹Losses by fire.

All profits go to stockholders.

The business for 1886, allowing the same rate of increase, ten per cent., as in recent years, was in all probability as much as $665,500 in the above ten companies.

Two companies outside of Massachusetts—at Nashua, N. H., and South Rygate, N. H., report a trade for 1886 of about $50,000, and returns as follows have been received from coöperative productive companies other than those in the above table, that were in business during all or part of 1886.

PRODUCTIVE COÖPERATION.

Name.	Location.	Capital.	No. of Shares.	No. of Shareholders.	No. of Workmen.	Date of Beginning Business.	Business in 1886.	Estimate of Business in 1887 based on business of Nov. to Jan. 1886-'87.	
Coöp. Granite Works of S. Ryegate.	South Ryegate, Vt.	$2,900	29	23	14	1885	$8,000	$8,000	All profits go to stockholders. Nine stockholders are workmen.
Rhode Island Coöp. Printing and Pub. Co.	Providence, R.I.	1,800	360	260	.....	1886	6,000¹	7,200	All profits go to stockholders. Labor organizations own part of stock.
S. Norwalk Coöp. Hat Co.	South Norwalk, Conn.	5,000¹	50	35	90	1885	30,000¹	30,000¹	All workmen must be stockholders. About one-third of workmen own stock.
Coöp. Iron Foundry	Nashua, N. H.	22,000	220	..	.....	1881	42,000	42,000	All profits above 6 per cent. interest on capital go henceforth to labor.
North Dighton Coöp. Stove Co.	Taunton, Mass.	11,500	175	27	22	July 1886	......	......	All profits go to stockholders. 17 workmen own stock.
Lynn K. of L. Coöp. Boot and Shoe Co.	Lynn, Mass.	8,000²	80	60	40	1886	35,000¹	60,000	About 35 workmen own stock. 10 per ct. of net profits go to K. of L.Assem. 45 per ct.net profits go to stockh'd'rs. 45 " " " workmen.
Spencer Coöp. Boot and Shoe Co.	Spencer, Mass.	6,200	620	100	15	1886	12,000¹	30,000	After payment of 6 per cent. interest on capital, and reserving 20 per ct. of net profits for sinking fund, rest goes to labor and capital in proportion borne by year's wages and cap'l.
Coöp. Printing and Pub. Co. of Boston	25 Beach street, Boston, Mass.	5,000	500	40	25	1886	......	......	10 per ct. net profits goes to labor. 5 " " " Dist.30.K of L. 10 " " is reserved as surplus. 25 " " for contingencies. 50 " " goes to propaganda.
Coöp. Granite Works	W. Quincy, Mass.	......	.....	...	...	1885	......	......	
Haverhill Printing and Pub. Co.	Haverhill, Mass.	......	.....	...	...		......	......	
Aggregate—10 Companies	......	$82,400	2,084	545	206		$133,000	$177,200	

¹Estimate by writer, where companies neglected to report and in one or two cases declined to make complete returns. In most cases, especially at Lynn and Spencer, the estimates are certainly not far from the truth. 2. Since increased to $10,000.

If we assume that the four companies from whom no return of trade has been obtained average a business of $13,000, or a total of $52,000, and one, the Coöperative Printing and Publishing Company of Boston, probably did a business of over $20,000, the entire business of the coöperative production in New England in 1886 may be safely estimated thus:

$665,500—as per previous table, increased
ten per cent from 1885.
133,000—business reported above.
52,000—business estimated.
————
$850,500—total business of twenty companies in 1886.

The present rate of business of these companies, joined to what may be done in the companies just organized, viz.: The K. of L. Coöp. Elastic Fabric Company of Chelsea; Scituate Coöp. Shoe Company, of Scituate, Mass.; Westboro Factory Association, of Westboro; K. of L. Coöp. Boot and Shoe Company, of Beverly, Mass., and the Brockton Coöp. Boot and Shoe Company, of Brockton, gives certain promise of a business exceeding $1,000,000 in 1887.

CREAMERIES.

The following creameries in Massachusetts were doing business in 1886. They were not minutely investigated, from lack of time and from the belief that they were of less moment than other classes of coöperative enterprises, although undoubtedly doing a good work, and, as a whole, prospering in it.

NAME.	LOCATION.	Capital.	Value of a Share.
Springfiield Coöp. Creamery..	Springfield, Mass..	$22,000	$20 00
Lowell Coöp Milk Asso........	Lowell, "	25,000	20 00
Amherst Coöp Creamery Asso.	Amherst, "	2,700	10 00
Berkshire Creamery Coöp Asso.	Sandisfield, "	1,400	25 00
Conway Coöp. Creamery Asso.	Conway, "	3,500	25 00
Cummington " " "	Cummington, "	2,500	25 00
Egremont " " "	Egremont, "	3,500	35 00
Hatfield " " Co:...	Hatfield, "	1,500	60 00
Hinsdale " " Asso.	Hinsdale, "	4,000	24 00
Rutland " " "	Rutland, "	2,000	10 00
Aggregate—10 Companies....................		$68,100	

The Amherst Company on a capital of $2,700 did a business of about $60,000 in 1886. It is probable all the above, together with coöperative creameries in the other New England States, did a business in 1886 of $500,000.

It is expected that the forthcoming report of the Massachusetts bank commissioners will reveal a business of $3,500,000. Certainly the coöperative banks of Massachusetts and the five or six of the other New England states have done that amount of business in 1886. The aggregate business of these various forms of coöperation in 1886 may be thus found:

Distributive coöperation did a business in 1886 of....... $2,000,000
Productive coöperation exclusive of creameries did a bus-
    iness in 1886 of...................................... 850,000
Creameries had a profit of............................. 500,000
Coöperative banks did a business of.................... 3,500,000

    Total... $6,850,000

Possibly, enough coöperative companies have been overlooked, or business underestimated in this investigation, to swell the total to $7,000,000. The coöperative business of New England in 1887 will surely reach $7,000,000.